CRCRCRCRCRCRCRCRCRCRCRCRCRCRCRCR

One Ordinary Woman,
One Extraordinary God

ଅ୪ଅ୪ଅ୪ଅ୪ଅ୪ଅ୪ଅ୪ଅ୪ଅ୪ଅ୪

One Ordinary Woman,
One Extraordinary God

LIFE ALTERING EXPERIENCES OF WOMEN

M Lorene Kimura

WESTBOW
PRESS
A DIVISION OF THOMAS NELSON

WestBow Press books may be ordered through booksellers or by contacting:

WestBow Press
A Division of Thomas Nelson
1663 Liberty Drive
Bloomington, IN 47403
www.westbowpress.com
1-(866) 928-1240

ISBN: 978-1-4497-5572-0 (sc)
ISBN: 978-1-4497-5573-7 (hc)
ISBN: 978-1-4497-5571-3 (e)

Library of Congress Control Number: 2012910281

Printed in the United States of America

WestBow Press rev. date: 8/6/2012

To the memory of
Florence (Flo) Emma Smawley

An incredible woman and prayer
warrior who loved and prayed me
into a wonderful relationship with Jesus

M Lorene Kimura

Lorene Kimura is very committed to helping women to find the freedom and to discover the special plan that God has just for them.

She encourages women of all ages through her speaking and teaching with messages full of biblical, practical realistic information tossed with a light dose of humour thrown in.

At the time of printing she has been a Christian for over 30 years and has been active in children's and women's ministry for much of that time. She is a graduate of the International School of Ministry (ISOM) with a diploma in Biblical Studies. She is also a graduate of the Wagner Institute with a Associates of Practical Ministry Diploma and is currently working on her Bachelor Diploma in the same.

She is a very proud wife, mother of two daughters, and of two granddaughters. Approximately three years ago Lorene added to her family when she found her birth family and now has a wonderful relationship with her younger sister.

In her free time she enjoys going for hikes with her camera and photographing nature and wildlife and has a collection of photos that she enjoys sharing and giving away to friends and family.

You can check her out at http://www.mlorenekimura.com.

രാരാരാരാരാരാരാരാരാരാരാരാരാരാരാരാ
This book belongs to:

_____

A woman God is calling
രാരാരാരാരാരാരാരാരാരാരാരാരാരാരാരാ

Acknowledgements

When God placed this work on my heart, I was not sure where it was going or who it was for. Was it for me or for the women of my church, or was it for those whom I had never met? I had no idea, but trying to be obedient to the leading of God, I proceeded. Now I cannot thank him enough for his guidance through this incredible experience.

After the first presentation of this book, which was at a women's retreat, Doris Lucas, a wonderful woman of God, told me to review it, because she believed that it would go on to reach others. I cannot thank her enough for the over 30 years of spiritual guidance that she has given me (even if I did not always want to hear what she was trying to say).

My pastor, John Lucas III, has been nothing but an encouragement to me. He allowed me the opportunity to work with him and for him for almost nine years while I lived in Calgary. During that time, he taught me so much about being in ministry. One thing I will always appreciate is how he showed enormous patience, never coming out and flatly rejecting any of my ideas, whether he agreed or not. He always got his point across by asking, "Did you consider this?" or, "What about that?" To top it off, his Sunday teachings were always educational, uplifting and challenging. He was always so real, saying, "I can only tell my story." Now, pastor, it is time for me to tell the story.

Elder Christopher has been a true mentor to me throughout this entire book-writing process, from the first time he personally shared the word of God and his life story with me, to the lunches where he challenged me, prophesied over me and constantly encouraged me. His wisdom has been brutally honest and has forced me to take a second look at this book and at myself, but he has also helped me to grow and, as a result, I have a greater understanding of the plan that God has for my life.

The first time I knew that I was to share these words; I envisioned an introductory skit for each woman. I knew no one better equipped than my good friend Gwen Vesterback. As usual, she was amazing, and she helped to make the weekend better than ever. As she read these women's stories, she encouraged me with her comments about how they have affected, challenged and uplifted her.

Janey Kinnley was able to read each page with a technical eye as well as a God-loving heart. She made suggestions, corrections and changes, and gave me her comments for possible "other thoughts." Her assistance was invaluable.

The women of Immanuel Church in Calgary, Alberta, Canada, have supported me as I tried to lead the women's ministry. They listened as I got on my soapbox about conferences and topics about which I felt very strongly and, in general, they were just there to support me. They were the ones who sat and listened as I presented this book over a two-day retreat. This group of women prayed for me and cried with me as well as laughed with and at me.

Don Enright (Don Enright Photography) and Tracey Heppner (tracey l heppner photography) both longtime friends, immediately offered to help when I called desperately looking for photographs. They both sent incredible photos, making it hard to decide which to use.

Last, but definitely not least, I want to thank my husband, Larry. He did not always understand what I was doing or why, but he never tried to discourage or stop me, and for that I thank him. At the end of the day, he was the one who had to give up our time together as I worked on this project.

Thank you all!

Contents

It should be that of your inner self, the unfading beauty of a gentle and quiet spirit, which is of great worth in God's sight.

1 Peter 3:4 (NIV)

Introduction

Ready, Set, Go!

Throughout the Bible, we find situations in which God was able to use people who, to our human eyes, should not, could not or would not be suitable instruments for his work. God was not interested in what society saw in these individuals' outside appearances, nor was he deterred by any label placed on them. What mattered to God was the fact that he called them for a purpose and they were willing to complete the task and serve him.

Today, many women look at their lives and fill their time with questions such as: Who am I? What meaningful thing could I possibly do? Who would ever want me? The answer to these questions can be found in the fact that God says you are priceless. He does not care about your past, but your future. He already knows everything you have done and everywhere you have been, but when you asked for his forgiveness, he took all of your sins and immediately erased them completely away. What he gave you back was a completely clean slate and the knowledge that he would always be there to help you along the way.

In Max Lucado's book for children, *You Are Special*, Eli, the master woodcrafter, tells little Punchinello, "You are special to me and I do not make mistakes." The message conveyed in this book is the same message that God has for you today—he does not make mistakes, and you are so very special. A friend sent me the following story by email. The message of the anonymous author holds true for so many women in our society.

By the time the Lord made woman, he was into his sixth day of working overtime. An angel appeared and said, "Why are you spending so much time on this one?"

The Lord answered, "Have you seen my spec sheet on her? She has to be completely washable but not plastic. She must have over 200 movable parts—all replaceable—and be able to run on Diet Coke and leftovers. She will have a lap that can hold four children at one time, a kiss that can cure anything from a scraped knee to a broken heart—and she will do everything with only two hands."

The angel was astounded at the requirements. "Only two hands? No way! That must be just on the standard model. That is too much work for one day. Wait until tomorrow to finish."

"But I will not," the Lord protested. "I am so close to finishing this creation that is so close to my own heart. She already heals herself when she is sick AND can work 18-hour days."

The angel moved closer and touched the woman. "But you have made her so soft, Lord."

"She is soft," the Lord agreed, "but I have also made her tough. You have no idea what she can endure or accomplish."

"Will she be able to think?" asked the angel.

The Lord replied, "Not only will she be able to think, she will be able to reason and negotiate."

The angel then noticed something, and reached out and touched the woman's cheek. "Oops, it looks like you have a leak in this model. I told you that you were trying to put too much into this one."

"That's not a leak," the Lord corrected, "that's a tear!"

"What's the tear for?" the angel asked.

The Lord said, "The tear is her way of expressing her joy, her sorrow, her pain, her disappointment, her love, her loneliness, her grief and her pride."

The angel was impressed. "You are a genius, Lord! You thought of everything! A woman is truly amazing."

And, she is! Women have strengths that amaze men. They bear hardships and they carry burdens, but they hold happiness, love and joy. They smile when they want to scream. They sing when they want to cry. They cry when they are happy and laugh when they are nervous. They fight for what they believe in. They stand up to injustice. They do not take "no" for an answer when they believe there is a better solution. They go without so their family can have. They go to the doctor with a frightened friend. They love unconditionally. They cry when their children excel and cheer when their friends get awards. They are happy when they hear about a birth or a wedding. Their hearts break when a friend dies. They grieve at the loss of a family member, yet they are strong when they think that there is no strength left. They know that a hug and a kiss can help to heal a broken heart. Women come in all sizes, colors and shapes. They will drive, fly, walk, run or send an e-mail to you to show how much they care about you. The hearts of women are what make the world keep turning! They bring joy and hope. They have compassion and ideals. They give moral support to their family and friends. Women have vital things to say and everything to give. However, if there is one flaw in women, it is that they tend to forget their worth.

The process you are now beginning will prove to be a great (and definitely eye-opening) adventure. As you reach the final pages, my prayer for each of you is that any flaw of poor self-worth you may have had will have completely vanished. I hope you will realize just how worthy you are to those around you and especially to God. When God calls on us to serve him, we can make up all kinds of excuses why we cannot or should not—"My kids are too young, so maybe when they are older," or, "My husband is not a Christian, and he just does not understand."

Personally, one of my favourite excuses is "Right now, I am too busy, but when things slow down then I will be able to focus." I recently heard a story from a 9/11 survivor who was recounting her time after escaping from the second tower. She told the story of how she witnessed to a young co-worker several times, but her response always came back the same. The co-worker said that she knew she needed to ask Jesus into her life, but always added, "Not now, it is something I will do when I am old and have finished everything else I want to do first." She almost missed her opportunity of "later."

God has given talents to each of us and we need to be ready to use them at a moment's notice. Ephesians 4:7 (NLT) says it very clearly: "However, he has given each one of us a special gift through the generosity of Christ." If you are willing to receive, he will send the Holy Spirit to be your guide along life's path to reach the purposes he has laid out for you. We do not have to have the best education or the most money, but we must be ready and willing to use what it is that we do have and believe that God will make a way for the rest.

A young girl presented her father with a gift that she had taken great love and time to prepare. To open his gift, he had to remove layer after layer after layer of wrapping paper, only to discover an empty box inside. The father became very upset with his daughter, reminding her that the paper was expensive and that she should not have wasted it. "But Daddy," she replied, "the box is not empty, I filled it with kisses."

The layers of outside wrapping paper were not important. It was the gift inside the box and the young girl's willingness to prepare the gift that counted. She knew that she had no money to buy a gift, but she was willing to use what she did have to provide her daddy a gift with love; we need to do the same for God. He does not care about your outside wrapping. He cares about what is in your heart.

At times, we complicate our lives and feel as if we have come too far down the highway named "demanding" to do any more. We see ourselves smashed up against a solid brick wall, unable to answer one more question, hear one more complaint or even take one more breath. Have images like this ever raced through your mind? Now is the time to change the picture of the brick wall into an image of God. Start to picture yourself pressed tightly against his heart, wrapped in his everlasting arms and soothed by his life-giving breath. Envision yourself encircled in God's love, soaked in his strength. Once you have done this, then, and only then, will you be ready to once again step back onto life's highway. Are you ready?

Jesus said to those who were with him that they needed to love one another as he loved them (John 15:12—NKJV). He also said that we were to minister to one another. He did not say "some" of you or that he would use "this" person but not "that" one—he said ALL of us are ministers. John 15:16 says, "You did not choose Me, but I chose you and appointed you that you should go and bear fruit and that your fruit should remain that whatever you ask the Father in My name He may give you" (NKJV).

Are you running from God or are you running to him? Are you waiting with an open heart and mind, telling him to use you in any way he desires? If your answer is yes, do you really mean it? If no, then ask God to help you to change your heart so that you can be able to work for him, and then keep reading to see how God used other women in the Bible.

Sometimes we find ourselves called to do tasks that are bigger than anything we could ever begin to imagine. Think of Noah's wife. Not much is written about her and we are never even told her name, but she knew that God was grieved by the way things were and that he was going to do something about it (Genesis 6:13). Maybe she caused her husband anguish as he was building the ark on dry land nowhere near an ocean: "Noah what are you doing? You are making us the laughingstock of the valley. Everyone is talking about you and they all think that this time you have really lost your mind!" She might have gone on and on; yet in her heart she must have known that Noah, the man she loved, had found favour with God. She knew that God would grant safety to him and his family (including her!) from the upcoming consequence of sin.

If she had not been a supporter of Noah and someone that God could use, I believe that God would have fashioned some way to exclude her from ever entering the ark. We only have to look as far as Lot's wife; she had one task, one instruction, "Do not look back!" Yet, her curiosity got the better of her and when it did, she immediately became a pillar of salt (Genesis 19:26).

Noah's wife was going to embark on the greatest adventure of her life. Still, she chose to follow, even though it was not always abundantly clear why they were doing some of the tasks asked of them. As each of us goes about our day-to-day routines, it is easy to fall into a rut; but a life with God at the helm will be an adventure if we allow it.

Luci Swindoll, once said, "Don't wait to live. Do not wait until you have more money or time. Do not wait until the kids are grown or you are out of debt. Do not wait until all the dishes match or the house is straight. Do not wait until both feet are on the ground. That day will never come. God has wonderful surprises for you this very minute if you will just let go of the things that are holding you back, and get involved."

Come, let us begin our journey as we look at the lives of women whom God can and did use. Some of these women you may immediately recognize, while you may have heard the names of others but know little more about them. You will soon discover that they all had very special qualities that God was able to use for his glory.

We will look at Sarah, who, though an old woman, was a person of great integrity who knew the expectations placed upon her. Mary, the mother of Jesus, was young but had an unfailing trust and instant willingness to serve God. Miriam started serving God as a young, fearless child and gave him her life, serving him through both good times and bad. The Woman at the Well was divorced several times but had the tenacity to ask questions. She also had a willingness to listen to the answers and learn. Abigail showed wisdom and was very giving, even to the point of offering herself for her husband's errors. The Widow of Zarephath and the Widow with Two Coins may not have had husbands; yet they continued to demonstrate love and trust in God.

We are warned not to get between a mother bear and her cubs because she will protect them until death, and that was the way it was for the Canaanite woman. Her child needed a touch from Jesus and she showed great perseverance to receive her daughter's healing. Lydia was a very successful businesswoman, but she knew the importance of witnessing and leading others she cared about to Jesus. Joanna was a very wealthy woman. She used her money to support Jesus and his work, always giving him her love and support.

Jesus can touch our hearts when we are not even really looking for him, just as the Widow of Nain discovered. Rahab desired to help God, even though it put her at great risk. In the end, she did not selfishly ask for safety and protection only for herself, but also for her family. All of us are sinners who at some point have fallen short of God's will for our lives. This can make us feel undesirable, but like the Sinful Woman who washed the feet of Jesus, if we humble ourselves before God, he will forgive us as we honour him.

Let's Pray

Lord, as we move into your Word and study these women's lives, help us to see what it is that they did that can help us as we walk with you. We will see and hear how you worked through them and used them no matter what their circumstances were.

Help us, Lord, to see that you can and want to use us no matter where we are right now, where we have been or what we have done. You have a plan and purpose for each of us and you want us to walk in it unafraid. You want us to be encouraged and empowered to take that first step just as a baby trusts her daddy as she learns to walk. It may not always turn out the way we want it to or think it should, but we know that you have our best interests in your hands. If we keep our eyes on you, we will move forward for you.

Help us, Lord, to use this lesson as a tool and to have the courage to move onward and upward for you. We thank you in advance, God, because with you nothing can stop us. Thank you, Lord, for the promptings you give directly through your Holy Spirit and for the ones you give to others to relay to us.

Is there anything too hard for the Lord?

Genesis 18:14 (NIV)

Never Give Up Hope

He used the old

(Genesis 17:15-23, 18:1-15)

S arah was over 90 years old when God fulfilled the promise that she would be the mother of nations and that Abraham would have offspring as numberless as the stars. Was Sarah perfect? No! Had she given up on God fulfilling his promise to her husband?

We know that Sarah became very impatient waiting for a child, even doubting that she ever would become pregnant; after all, she was now an old woman. So she thought she would help God and devise her own version of his plan. She talked Abraham into being with Hagar, which resulted in the conception of his son Ishmael (Genesis 16:3-4). To top it off, when the angel said that she was going to have a child of her own, she laughed and said, "An old woman like me? Get pregnant? With this old man of a husband?" (Genesis 18:12 MSG).

We know that God has a plan for us, but when we feel it is not happening fast enough, we have a strong urge to design our own fulfillment of that plan. We feel we can accelerate the process and reach the goal we have decided is perfect for us. Next, we start to "pray our methods," giving God the instructions and details we have developed for ourselves. There is an old saying: If you want to give God a good laugh, just tell Him your plans! I think God sometimes leaves the door open for us to try our own approaches so that he can prove to us that our ways are not his ways. He lets us try and lets us fail—not to hurt us, but rather, so that we can learn. In the end, we become stronger in him, having learned that we really do need to rely on him.

Have you ever heard a parent say to her child, "If you think you can do it better, then go ahead and try!"? The parent may let her child make an attempt, but she is usually in the background, watching and ready to catch the child if he fails. God is like that; he is always there with his loving, never-condemning arms to pick us up. When my daughter was in junior high, she told me that I could not always protect her and that sometimes she would have to fail and make her own mistakes. This is a hard lesson for a parent to learn because no parent wants to see his or her child hurting. God does not want to see us hurt either, but he is willing to let us fail if it will put us back on the right path and make us stronger than ever.

The doubt that Sarah felt changed to fear when she heard a stranger ask her, "Is there anything too hard for God?" (Genesis 18:14 MSG). We need to have faith and trust in God and his plan for us even though our human emotions will try to take over and rule us. All of Sarah's emotions were right on the surface—fear, doubt, impatience and/or inadequacy—the same feelings we often experience as well. In the end, just as she did, we must place our trust, faith and hope in God.

At age 65, an age at which we would expect to look forward to maybe slowing down and retiring, Sarah was just beginning a new adventure. Abraham had asked her to leave her home to follow him along God's roadmap to some faraway place where she would know no one. It must have been very difficult for her to leave everything familiar behind and to start over with nothing, but she went because she trusted God.

It is important that we learn to trust God in all things. "God assured us, 'I'll never let you down, never walk off and leave you,' we can boldly quote, 'God is there, ready to help; I'm fearless no matter what. Who or what can get to me?'" (Hebrews 13:5 MSG). When life's trials come, we need to remember that it may seem like there is no light at the end of the tunnel, but God is there and he is our light. "God is a safe place to hide; ready to help when we need him" (Psalm 46:1 MSG). In Isaiah 41:10 it says, "Do NOT fear for I am with you, Do NOT be dismayed because I am your God, I will strengthen you, I will help you, I will uphold you with my righteous right hand" (NKJV). This one scripture provides us with five powerful reasons why we never need to be fearful:

1. He very plainly says that he is with us and that we are never alone, so do not fear in taking the step of faith to follow him.

2. He says that we need not be troubled because he is our God and that there is no other like him.

3. He promises that he will be our strength when we feel that we do not have an ounce of strength left.

4. He says very simply that he will help us.

5. Finally, he says that he will uphold us with his righteous right hand.

Why should we ever worry when, in just one verse, he so plainly and clearly gives us all these reasons not to fear? In fact, "do not fear" appears over 150 times in the King James Bible.

Sarah finally trusted God and let him work in her life, even though she was old in the eyes of the world. Some believe that she was too old to even still be alive, let alone to have a child and become the mother of nations; and yet, she was not too old for God. Sarah trusted God to do what he said he would do; she knew deep in her heart that her God could do anything. She rested (trusted) on the word that her God would bring to pass whatever he had said he would. When Sarah heard that she would be a mother at 90 years old, she could not help but laugh.

Think of it—any of you who are 50 years or older, what would you do if you were told that you were going to have a child? And for those of you under 50, try to imagine being told that you will have a baby in 10, 15 or 20 years. I know I would want to run and hide as fast and as far away as I possibly could. After having a grandchild, I fully understand the statement that having children is for the young. I no longer have the

3

energy to constantly chase, change, get up in the middle of the night or do everything else that is required for a child day in and day out. If I were 90 years old, it would have to be by the grace of God, because it surely could not and would not be of my own strength.

Sarah was a woman of integrity. She knew her position and the expectations placed on her. Now, all of you who want to bring women out of the kitchen settle down, because I am not saying that she was a doormat. Sarah was a spiritual role model. She loved Abraham and wanted to follow him and be with him no matter what. In one of my favourite books of the Bible, 1 Peter, I read, "they without a word, may be won by the conduct of their wives" (3:1). It goes on in verses 3-4 to say, "Do not let your adornment be merely outward—arranging the hair, wearing gold, or putting on fine apparel—[4] rather let it be the hidden person of the heart, with the incorruptible beauty of a gentle and quiet spirit, which is very precious in the sight of God." We can accomplish much by simply obeying God and following his Word. We do not have to be loud and vocal activists, but merely loving servants of God, doing what he tells us through his Holy Spirit. We can be bold and courageous, yet still be obedient. The words God spoke to Joshua, "Be strong and of good courage; do not be afraid, nor be dismayed, for the LORD your God is with you wherever you go" Joshua 1:9 (NKJV) demonstrate how much truth and power we, as women, have if we are only bold enough and strong enough. Know that the Lord God is with us to help us; he will uphold us as we go through whatever it is that he has in store for us.

The roadmap for Sarah did not always lead along a smooth and easy path as she waited for God to fulfill his Word. To begin with, she had to leave her family and home and then pretend that she was Abraham's sister instead of his wife. She felt that she had to help God along by having her husband, the man she loved; sleep with another woman, only to see Hagar give birth to her husband's first son, which was something Sarah had longed to do herself. Then, the son she longed for arrived; but why did it have to be at 90 years old? It only goes to show that God does have a sense of humour; maybe that is why her son's name was *Isaac*—"one who laughs." The final straw was when Sarah overheard Ishmael poking fun at her precious son, Isaac. That was more than she could bear, and she forced Abraham to banish his own flesh and blood, Ishmael, and his mother, Hagar, from his home.

Turn Your Heart

God has planted dreams in our hearts, some of which may seem impossible to us, but remember, nothing is impossible with God.

What dreams have you put off because you have been too afraid or too busy to follow them or because they just seemed too large to happen?

I encourage you to write your dreams, ideas and desires in your journal and then turn them over to God, trusting him to bring them to pass if he has so planned.

Let's Pray

Lord, you have a plan and purpose for each of us, one you designed long before we were born. We have this promise confirmed with the words you spoke to Jeremiah, "For I know the plans I have for you, declares the LORD, plans to prosper you and not to harm you, plans to give you hope and a future" (Jeremiah 29:11 NIV).

Help us to erase our impatience, our fear and our doubt then have them replaced with a new and strong trust in you. You are the author and the finisher of each of the dreams you have placed in our hearts and you are the one who can make them happen. Help us to be bold and strong while being obedient as we wait upon your Word. Help us to know when it is you who are speaking to us through the Holy Spirit and when it is our very overactive imaginations. We want to follow the path that you have set for us so that we can be the best in you and for you that we can be. With your direction, we can do it. Thank you, Lord, for your guidance and your love.

Future Study Scriptures

📖 Numbers 12:6   📖 Jeremiah 32:37
📖 1 Chronicles 28:19   📖 Daniel 1:17
📖 Psalm 33.11   📖 Daniel 5:12
📖 Proverbs 16:9   📖 Joel 2:28
📖 Proverbs 19:21   📖 Luke 1:837

Additional Analysis

For further investigation, read Genesis 17:15-3, 8:1-15

1. *Sarah* and *Sarai* mean "princess," which suits a mother of nations. Do you know the meaning of your name? If not, try looking it up on the Internet or in a baby name book. Do you think the meaning has relevance to your life?

2. How do you think Sarah felt about herself when it seemed like God would not be giving her a son after he had promised Abraham that he would be the father of nations?

3. How did Sarah interpret God's silence?

4. Has there been a time in your life when you felt God's silence as Sarah did? How did you interpret it?

5. What was Sarah's reaction when she discovered that her plan was not working the way she had designed it?

6. How did her interpretation influence the rest of her life?

7. Sarah laughed at the announcement that she was going to have a baby. How do you think you would have reacted in her situation?

8. What emotions may Sarah have experienced when she discovered that she was pregnant?

9. What do you think was the biggest test of Sarah's faith?

10. What evidence is there that she experienced real low points?

11. What does Hebrews 13:5 mean to you? *(Refer to our text to read it as it was written in the Message translation.)

12. Find and list here at least five other scriptures that tell us not to fear. What do these scriptures tell us about God?

13. God knows your thoughts, your fears and your dreams. Does this comfort you or does it put you on edge? Why?

14. When you look at the following scriptures, do you believe there is anything too hard for our God?
    a. Genesis 18:14
    b. Jeremiah 32:27
    c. Luke 1:37
    d. Luke 18:27

Memory Verse

"Be strong and be brave, don't be afraid and don't be frightened because the Lord thy God will go with you. He will not leave you or forget you" (Deuteronomy 31:6 NCV).

Newfound Facts

_____

_____

_____

_____

Psalm 139 (MSG)

¹GOD investigate my life; get all the facts firsthand.

²I am an open book to you; even from a distance, you know what I am thinking.

³You know when I leave and when I get back; I am never out of your sight.

⁴You know everything I am going to say before I start the first sentence.

⁵I look behind me and you're there, then up ahead and you're there, too—your reassuring presence, coming and going.

⁶This is too much, too wonderful—I can't take it all in!

⁷Is there anyplace I can go to avoid your Spirit? To be out of your sight?

⁸If I climb to the sky, you're there! If I go underground, you're there!

⁹If I flew on morning's wings to the far western horizon,

¹⁰You'd find me in a minute—you're already there waiting!

¹¹Then I said to myself, "Oh, he even sees me in the dark! At night I'm immersed in the light!"

¹²It's a fact: darkness isn't dark to you; night and day, darkness and light, they're all the same to you.

¹³Oh yes, you shaped me first inside, then out; you formed me in my mother's womb.

¹⁴I thank you, High God—you're breathtaking! Body and soul, I am marvellously made!

I worship in adoration——what a creation!

¹⁵You know me inside and out, you know every bone in my body; You know exactly how I was made, bit by bit, how I was sculpted from nothing into something.

¹⁶Like an open book, you watched me grow from conception to birth; all the stages of my life were spread out before you, the days of my life all prepared before I'd even lived one day.

¹⁷Your thoughts—how rare, how beautiful! God, I'll never comprehend them!

¹⁸I couldn't even begin to count them—any more than I could count the sand of the sea.

Oh, let me rise in the morning and live always with you!

¹⁹And please, God, do away with wickedness for good! And you murderers—out of here!

²⁰All the men and women who belittle you, God, infatuated with cheap god-imitations.

²¹See how I hate those who hate you, GOD, see how I loathe all this godless arrogance;

²²I hate it with pure, unadulterated hatred. Your enemies are my enemies!

²³Investigate my life, O God, find out everything about me; Cross-examine and test me, get a clear picture of what I'm about;

²⁴See for yourself whether I've done anything wrong—then guide me on the road to eternal life.

❧ And now, Israel, what does the LORD your God require of you, but to fear the LORD your God, to walk in all His ways and to love Him, to serve the LORD your God with all your heart and with all your soul. ❧

Deuteronomy 10:12 (NKJV)

2

Loving and Trusting

He used the young

(Matthew 1-2; 12:46-50, Luke 1-2; 8:19-21)

Mary was still a young teen when she was given the honour of becoming the mother of Jesus. God looked at her and saw something in her that nobody else could see; she was a young woman whom he could use because she loved and trusted him and was willing to serve him (Acts 13:22). There was nothing particularly special about her upbringing. She was not a princess or a socialite's daughter; actually, she was just an ordinary small-town girl.

Mary did everything that was expected of a young 15-year-old girl of her time. She worked, grinding the barley into flour, baking the bread and preparing dishes of beans, veggies, eggs, fruits, nuts and sometimes mutton. She helped to make wool into clothing and, of course, in such a small village there was the constant caring for the many young children. Like the Woman at the Well, she had to go and fetch water for washing and cooking. In fact, in Nazareth today, there is a well referred to as "Mary's Well." Even though she was such a "regular" girl, we know for sure that God wanted her. Luke 1:28 says "Rejoice, highly favored one, the Lord is with you; blessed are you among women!" (NKJV).

Mary loved God so much that she never even thought to say no to him. She simply said yes according to his Word. The trust and faith that she had in God and her obedience to him must have been insurmountable. Think about it, what would you do if an angel appeared to tell you that you would be the mother of Jesus? Can you even begin to imagine what it must have been like? Think of the emotions that would immediately flood over your entire being—emotions of fear, confusion, disbelief, unworthiness and self-questioning regarding why God would ever think to choose you. I am sure that Mary may have felt all of this in the first few seconds, but just as quickly as they entered, they were replaced with overwhelming joy and peace, followed by an incredible thankfulness, awe and a very passionate desire to serve.

But the angel Gabriel said to her, "Do not be afraid, Mary; you have found favor with God. You will conceive and give birth to a son, and you are to call him Jesus. He will be great and will be called the Son of the Most High." (Luke 1:30-32 NIV). The angel Gabriel's message struck her like a lightning bolt, but still she was quick to answer with faith and humility. Her direct and confident "Yes" made her one of the first modern disciples. She never said, "Oh, let me go and discuss it with my family or with Joseph." Instead, she immediately responded, choosing obedience and simply answering, "Yes."

We may not know a lot about Mary, but we do know that she was a young woman of great faith who continued to live her life by faith. Mary was known as a maidservant or handmaiden, which means that she was an eager and willing slave. Mary knew her will was not her own but that of her master. She knew, as a handmaiden, that she was to obey without question and she accepted that. Knowing and believing this, Mary obeyed God's will for her life even though this one decision of obedience would change her life forever.

Being young, Mary was unaccomplished and had not yet really had an opportunity to live. She had taken care of children but never gone through the experience of childbirth and becoming a mother. She had no social status; she was very poor, which meant there would be no inheritance from her family. Some even say that she was not particularly pretty. Now she was not only unmarried, but unmarried and pregnant. She would have gone through a great deal of ridicule and been labelled a fornicator, a bad person and the kind of girl a mother warns her sons to avoid. She was not the one you would be excited to have all your friends discover was to be the mother of YOUR grandchild. Yet, God saw something different; he saw what her parents had instilled in her—a genuine love for him.

Mary believed Joseph when he told her that God spoke to him in his dreams, and she was very open and obedient to her husband's direction. She followed him, leaving everything and everyone to sneak away in the night and escape to Egypt to prevent Herod from killing her son. Two years later, after Joseph said he had another dream, she followed him back again. How do you think you would react? Would you immediately want to follow without question if your husband came and said, "I have had a dream, and this is what I think we should do?" (When I told someone I know and respect that I had a feeling I was to complete this study on women for women, the person asked me if I was hallucinating!) Yet, Mary knew that God was speaking to her husband. It was no hallucination and she was willing to follow. Mary was a true believer through and through!

Right away, Mary's experiences tell us that, as far as God is concerned, it does not matter what our backgrounds are. It does not matter how rich or poor we are or how successful we are, but it does matter what is in our hearts. When God is calling, he looks deep into our hearts to see who we really are and what is making us tick.

There have been times when I've looked at my life and thought, "Oh, God, I cannot believe that you have allowed me to minister to your women." Ministry was not a path that I thought I would ever end up taking. Not so many years ago, I had my own fund-raising company, was working and had written a "how to" book after graduating from Volunteer Sector Management with a Fund Raising major. I had it made; I was on my way! God, though, had another plan, and through circumstances that we might think horrible—two car accidents—God brought me to himself, leading me in a new direction, one in which I now cannot imagine not going.

We need to make it our heart's first and foremost desire to develop and feed a deep obedient love for God, one that may forever change the path we have planned for our lives.

When God looked for the perfect person, he chose one we might consider unlikely, but whom he said was perfect. She was young, but willing, and God used her!

This episode was just the first of many times that God was able to work through Mary. As Jesus grew up and Mary aged, she experienced each of the seasons that Jesus went through with all of the emotions of any mother. There must have been an overwhelming joy as she followed and watched Jesus teaching in his Father's name. Can you not just feel the excitement she must have felt as she witnessed his first miracle when he turned water into wine at that wedding? Imagine the joy turning to horror and a devastating grief when she witnessed what they did to him—as they whipped him, beat him, humiliated him, hated him and then brutally hung him on the cross. Or, on the day of his resurrection, when she realized he was alive, overwhelming joy must have once again encompassed her heart.

She knew that he was the Son of God and not her son, but there was still a strong bond because God had allowed her to carry him in her womb for nine months and raise him as her own son. He had allowed her to feel him as an unborn child kicking and moving inside her. He had allowed her to give birth to Jesus, hold him, nurture him and love him as an infant, in childhood and then as a young man. Through all of this, Mary continued to love God and wanted to serve him in any way that he would ask. Mary went through all of the real emotions that we feel—real problems, real fears and real failings, but God was able to use her to accomplish his will because of her willing heart. We look to Mary and honour her for her faith, but Matthew 12:50 states, "For whoever does the will of my Father in heaven is my brother and sister and mother" (NLT).

Turn Your Heart

We would have to call Mary's life an adventure: her encounter with an angel, the pregnancy and birth of Jesus, the childhood of Jesus, his adult life and crucifixion and, finally, the resurrection and ascension. Think of what it must have been like for her to be in the upper room with Jesus' closest friends on earth as the Holy Spirit arrived with tongues of fire.

What are your struggles?

What are your joys?

Ask the Holy Spirit to come and reveal to you how to use these struggles and joys for God's glory.

Delve into the scriptures; ask God to give you a deeper understanding of what it is that he has planned for your life.

Pray for the grace to be more like Mary, who obediently said, "I am the Lord's servant. May it be to me as you have said" (Luke 1:38 NIV).

Let's Pray

Lord, you chose Mary, not because of what she had done or which family she was from, but because of her genuine heart and love for you. I want to have that kind of genuine heart of love, one in which people can see you. Lord, I want to be a person in whom you can see the heart of a servant who really wants to serve you and your people. Lord, as Kathy Troccolli sings in her song, "You Are the Heart of Me," "Teach me to love like you love, teach me to live, as you would have me live. Teach me to feel like you feel, teach me to hope like you hope. You are the light revealing every part of me; you are the heart of me." It is you and me, God; with you in control, we can do anything. Use me, Lord.

Future Study Scripture

- 📖 Deuteronomy 6:5
- 📖 Deuteronomy 10:12
- 📖 Joshua 22:5
- 📖 Joshua 23:11
- 📖 Nehemiah 1:5
- 📖 Psalm 45:7
- 📖 Psalm 70:4
- 📖 Ecclesiastes 9:1
- 📖 Amos 5:15
- 📖 Micah 6:8
- 📖 Zephaniah 3:17
- 📖 Matthew 6:24
- 📖 Mark 12:30
- 📖 Luke 10:27
- 📖 John 3:16

Additional Analysis

For further investigation, read Matthew 1-2; 12:46-50, Luke 1-2. 8; 19-21, Luke 45-56, Joshua 22:5, Matthew 22:37, Mark 12:33

1. Many of us have had special people influence our lives. What does being a role model mean to you? Who are your role models and what makes them so special? Are any of them teens or much younger than you are?

2. How do you think you would react if the angel Gabriel came to you as he did to Mary? What do you think would be your response?

3. If God sent an angel to you right now, what kind of message do you think he would deliver? What would this message tell you about yourself and what would it say about the rapport between you and God?

4. Many people today think that obedience reflects a form of control by another. What does obedience mean to you?

5. From Mary's reaction, what do we see about her relationship with God?

6. How would you like to see your relationship grow with God?

7. What outcomes can we generate for ourselves by not believing in God's promises?

8. Mary's life changed drastically after her response to God. In what ways do you see it becoming harder?

9. In Luke 1:28, Mary is called "highly favoured." What do you think it would be like if you were called "highly favoured"?

10. Why do you think God selected Mary to be the mother of Christ? After all, she was young, inexperienced and not very well off.

11. What God is asking of Mary is going to be very difficult for her, yet she also realizes that God is honouring her by giving her a major role in his plan for humanity (Luke 1:18-49). Try to describe an experience in which you have been called to do something that is an honour yet very difficult.

12. Does looking back at Mary's life and knowing how faithful God was to her help you to move on in his plan for your life? Why or why not?

Memory Verse

"You love right and hate evil, so God has chosen you from among your friends. He has set you apart with much joy" (Psalm 45:7 NCV).

Newfound Facts

_____

_____

_____

_____

_____

_____

_____

_____

_____

M Lorene Kimura

_____

_____

_____

_____

_____

_____

_____

_____

_____

_____

_____

_____

_____

_____

_____

_____

_____

❧ Joy in Forgiveness of Israel's Sins—Praise the LORD! Oh, give thanks to the LORD, for He is good! For His mercy endures forever. ❧

Psalm 106:1(NKJV)

3

A Lifelong Mission

God used the unmarried

(Exodus15, Numbers12)

Miriam's first encounter with God was when he used her in a mighty way when she was very young. Throughout her life, she continued to experience God as he worked out the details of his plan for her. Her life is a wonderful example of how best to live your life as well as how not to live it. Her actions demonstrated examples of true forthright courage, faith and an ability to think very quickly on her feet. Yet, her life also reveals to us what can happen if we do not follow the plan God has intended for us or if we try to undermine his authority or the authority that he has given to others.

God was able to use Miriam as a child. As she grew, she developed into a prophetess who spoke God's Word to many. She, alongside her brothers, Moses and Aaron, was a true leader to her people.

Throughout her life, she was a visionary/prophetess, a witness, a worshipper/worship leader and, in her disobedience, she acted as a warning and an example of God's magnificent grace. As a visionary or a prophetess, Miriam displays how we must stay on our toes and be ready for our appointed times. As a witness, she saw many miracles, such as shoes that never wore out and God supplying the provisions for day-to-day living in the wilderness. She saw and heard the sea roll back as God separated it for their great escape. As a worshipper and a worship leader, she led a dance and composed a song as they came across the opened sea, only to have the same sea close again and roll back on the enemy soldiers. Finally, she felt the admonishment of God, revealing what can happen when we criticize and demean those that God has placed into leadership. Yet, God's wonderful grace and mercy broke through to shower blessings on her as she sought forgiveness.

The first time that we hear of Miriam she is only 12 years old. We read about her extraordinary love for her family and an extra special spot in her heart for her little brother, Moses. Miriam wanted to help to protect him or, at the very least, watch over him as long as she could. This was difficult because Pharaoh had passed a decree for the immediate murder of all newborn boys (Exodus 1:22). She helped her mother to hide and nurture her little brother in their home until he was too big to hide any longer. When Jochebed placed her infant son amongst the bulrushes, she had no idea what would be in store for him. Miriam, being a very protective big sister, stayed back and watched (Exodus 2:4), still trying to look out for her little brother.

When Pharaoh's daughter came and rolled the reeds back to reveal baby Moses, Miriam took the initiative to approach her with an offer to help her find someone to be a nursemaid to the baby. Of course, she ran and told her mom, who was then able to take Moses back and safely care for him; after all, it was now for the Pharaoh's daughter, not herself. Their family even received a bonus, because they paid Miriam's mother for her services. This was the first of many times that Moses was responsible for helping his family. Miriam was a very precocious child who showed such love, caring, compassion and devotion to her family that she was able to help save the life of her younger brother. She had no way of knowing that her actions would later result in Moses being used to save her people.

The Bible never recorded whether or not Miriam ever married, but scholars think that she remained single and presented her life as an opportunity for God to use it as he saw fit. Miriam became one of the strongest female leaders in the Bible, alongside her brothers, Aaron and Moses (Micah 6:4). She was a major contributor, as were her brothers, and she led the Israelites across the Red Sea (Exodus 15:20). Here, she would lead the worship and speak God's word to his people. Exodus 15:21 "Sing to the Lord, for He is highly exalted. The horse and its rider He has hurled into the sea" (NKJV).

Even though Miriam trusted, loved and honoured God, the green monster of envy appeared, rearing its ugly head. She became very upset with always playing second fiddle to her brother Moses. She and her brother Aaron started to question God's judgment in making Moses the leader when they thought they could do just as good or even better a job.

God has given gifts/talents to each of us that we need to recognize and ensure that we use properly. Ephesians 2:10 reads, "He creates each of us by Christ Jesus to join him in the work he does, the good work he has gotten ready for us to do, work we had better be doing" (MSG). We must always be very conscious of where these gifts have come from and not let them go to our heads as they did with Miriam. We do not want to get into a situation as she did, forcing God's hand to deal with us to bring us back to earth.

There is a difference between knowing that God has given you a gift that you are good at and bragging about it. The first time I told my daughter that I really enjoyed fund raising and was good at it. She told me I sounded like a braggart and that I was being snobby, but I told her we all have gifts and one of mine is being able to do this job and do it well. I also knew who allowed me to do it and to be successful at it. It was not me, myself or I, but God.

Miriam made a huge mistake when she questioned God's choice of Moses as the leader. Later, she was forced to endure the consequences of those actions. For one week, Miriam had to undergo the pain and suffering of leprosy. God, who is a God filled with grace and mercy, loved her too much to leave her there as she repented. He healed her and returned her to once again serve him—yes, under the leadership of Moses. Inflicting Miriam with leprosy turned her into a walking dead woman. Leprosy meant complete isolation. Lepers were outcasts from their family, friends and everyone else, except those who had the same disease. There was very little worse than being labelled a leper and being forced to live in a colony with other lepers. God left her there for a time. In those days, there was no cure of three little pills to take each day as we often hear about in advertisements on television.

God may allow us to experience trials for a season, even though we question why we must endure them. For us, these trials feel like the darkest times of our lives and nothing else could ever be worse. I am not going to be like Job's so-called friends and say all you need to do is confess the sin in your life and everything will be okay. Rather, I am here to say that with every pain and every hurt, we need to keep our eyes focused on Jesus and remember that he took them to the cross for us. That is not to say we should make light of pain or suffering, or forego trying to understand why good people have to go through hard times. What we do need to remember is that, through it all, Jesus is there for us and we need to call out continually to him.

I do believe that sometimes God has to let us go through trying times to get our attention. Another reason can be for us to learn a lesson we are going to need in the future to minister to others going through similar experiences. Consider John 9:3 (the story of the blind man who Jesus healed with spit and dirt): "Jesus answered, 'Neither this man nor his parents sinned, but that the works of God should be revealed in him'" (NKJV). This young man did nothing wrong, nor did he ask to be blind, but when Jesus healed him, he was able to empathize with others who were blind. He could also attest with conviction and knowledge to the true miracles of God.

One of the original Women of Faith speakers, Barbara Johnson, is a great example of someone who went through severe hardship. When you read her story, you wonder why she had to undergo so much or how she ever managed it. She found what she thought was a deer lying dead on the road, only to discover that it was her husband, who was near death. As a result of the car accident, he lost his sight and the ability to care for himself until one day when God completely healed him. She had four sons. One week before one of her sons was to return home from Vietnam, he took a bullet and died. Another son, on his way home from Alaska, died when a drunk driver hit his car, his death five years to the day after the death of the first son. She was estranged from her third son for many years after she discovered his involvement in a gay lifestyle.

Just as everything seemed to be going well once again, the doctor discovered a brain tumour infiltrating Barbara's body, for which she had to have surgery and a great many follow-up treatments. If that was not enough, her husband, who had been her earthly rock, passed away.

How can one person take all of this, and why should one person have to? We do not know why, but we do know that she did survive. Through it all, a thriving ministry called Spatula Ministries was born, and even after the doctors told Barbara that she could not travel great distances, she continues her work helping parents through the shock of finding out that their child is gay.

Whatever trial life tossed at Barbara, she reacted like the punching bag that kids play with that pops back up when you punch it down. Her brain tumour and her husband's death could not keep her down, although they changed her life dramatically. What did not change was her love for God and his people and her wonderful sense of healing humour. After losing her second son and then becoming estranged from her third, she tells the story of how she considered suicide by driving off the viaduct, stopping only because she was afraid that she would not die and would end up maimed. It was also there that she was finally able to say, "Whatever, Lord." Those two words changed her life forever. Barbara Johnson believed in those words and lived true to them until her death in July 2007.

God, whatever you have planned for me, I can do it as long as we are together—no matter if it is illness, hardship or whatever other trial that may come my way.

I can only guess that Miriam did not start her week of illness and banishment by saying "Whatever, Lord." For an entire week, she had time to think, to cry out to God, to repent and to relearn leaning on him, not herself. Miriam's punishment may also have been a wakeup call for the Israelites to recognize that their sin was threatening the unity of the entire group. Perhaps they realized that if this could happen to

Miriam, a strong woman of God and a prophetess, then who were they to think that they would be forever protected from the consequences of their actions? God's plan for Miriam was not to leave her in that situation, but for her to learn a very important lesson. He restored her completely, and when she returned, she had a new attitude toward God and the plan he had for her. I believe that she shared the messages of hope in God and obedience to God loudly and clearly with the Israelites.

Sometimes it can be difficult for us to look at our leaders and not think that we could do a better job, but it is vital to understand that God has a unique and special call on each of our lives. Remember, we will be judged accordingly for the talents that we have been given and what we do with them. Ecclesiastes 12:14 says, "For God will bring every deed into judgment, including every secret thing, whether good or evil" (NKJV). In addition, when we look at the leaders we know, if they are not doing as instructed by God, he, not we, will judge them. James 3:1 tells us that: My brethren, let not many of you become teachers, knowing that we shall receive a stricter judgment" (NKJV). If you want God to trust you with more, you must first be content and do the best you can with the talents that he initially gives you.

The parable of three men with talents appears in Matthew 25:14-28. The "talents" referred to in this parable are not personal talents, but rather, they refer to the currency of that day. Even so, when we read this story, we can see how the individuals did or did not use their money and how important it is that we use whatever we have—money or personal talent—to the best of our ability.

One man received five talents. He used them the best he could and was honoured by having them doubled. A second man was given two talents. He also used them the best he could and his talents were doubled as well. However, the third man, who was given one talent, hid it away and then tried to blame his lack of increase on the master, saying that he knew that he was a hard taskmaster, thus causing him to be afraid of losing that one talent. His reward included having his talent completely taken away, being called lazy and being sent away (Matthew 25:14-26). The first two men were honoured and rewarded with a doubling of their talents, while the third man, because of his general laziness, was stripped of all that he had been given.

No matter how tough we feel our trials are, we need to make the best of them. Through it all, remember the words of the amazing Barbara Johnson—"Whatever, Lord!" Try to say them out loud where you are right now: "Whatever, Lord!"

Turn Your Heart

If someone like Miriam the prophetess must suffer consequences for rebelling and questioning God, who are we to think the good works of our past will carry us through our present disobedience?

Take time in prayer and ask God to reveal to you the things in your life that are displeasing to him.

Write them in your prayer journal, **really** turn them over to God and ask his forgiveness so that you can move on under his leadership and not have any shadows pulling at you from behind.

Be honest with yourself, because God already knows the things in your life that are displeasing to him and is just waiting for you to come honestly to him.

We all have jobs to do and positions to hold, just as Miriam discovered, and to complete God's plan, we must each do our part. Romans 12:4-13 tells us exactly this. In verse 6 we read, "We all have different gifts, each of which came because of the grace God gave us" (NCV). The exercises in the Additional Analysis can open new doors for you to do the work God has planned for you. Using the talents he has given you will result in feeling contentment and joy, knowing you are serving God the best you can. If, after completing the exercise, you still feel confused, turn it over to God and ask him for help. James 1:5-6 says, "If any of you lacks wisdom, he should ask God, who gives generously to all without finding fault, and it will be given to him. But when he asks, he must believe and not doubt, because he who doubts is like a wave of the sea, blown and tossed by the wind" (NIV).

God may have a surprise for you as to what gifts he would like to see you using. The first time I completed a study on my giftings, like everyone else around me, I thought I knew for sure what my strongest gift would be. I soon discovered that gift was actually secondary in my life and there was one stronger that I had not put into use as I could have. As we grow in Christ, our giftings may change in priority; I know that mine definitely have. With that in mind, I recommend repeating the gifting exercise every few years. It is also a great confirmation to see what God is doing in your life.

Let's Pray

God, you are a God of grace and mercy, and I thank you and praise you. I know that you love me too much to leave me as I am. I ask you now to help me to see the errors of my ways and I will be quick to repent so that I do not have to stay on the outside looking in. I thank you, Lord, for the joy that comes with your forgiveness. I thank you, God, that you have given me talents to use for your glory. Help me to learn what they are and to start walking in them with courage and a new boldness that comes from you. With you at the head, God, we can do anything.

Future Study Scriptures

📖 Deuteronomy 28:1
📖 Ezra 3:11
📖 Psalm 106:1
📖 Daniel 9:9
📖 Chronicles 16:34
📖 2 Chronicles 12:7

📖 Jeremiah 33:11
📖 Mark 10:47
📖 Luke 11:10
📖 Luke 24:53
📖 Romans 9:15

Additional Analysis

For further investigation, read Exodus 15 and Numbers 12

1. Miriam is an example of how God can use an unmarried woman. Has a single woman influenced your life or your church? If yes, how?

2. What characteristics or personality traits do you see in Miriam?

3. How important was Miriam's role in her brother's future?

4. Miriam had a very special position among her people. What was it?

5. Miriam demonstrated a very powerful method of worship after crossing the Red Sea. Why do you think she chose dance as her expression to show her appreciation?

6. What is the significance of the instrument—the timbrels—that Miriam used to lead her dance?

7. In what ways do we demonstrate worship to God today?

8. How did Miriam react under Moses' leadership?

9. What did Moses do that made Miriam and Aaron angry enough to start a mutiny?

10. What were the consequences of Miriam's actions?

11. Why do think that only Miriam experienced punishment when Aaron was guilty too?

12. Do you think that Miriam's punishment had an effect on Aaron? If so, what?

13. What do the following scriptures teach us about criticizing others and overestimating our own importance?

    a. Proverbs 30:12
    b. Luke 18:11
    c. Romans 12:3
    d. Philippians 2:3–4

14. In what ways has God gifted you to serve others in your family, your church and your community?

15. What have you learned from Miriam's example?

16. How does Miriam influence your future life?

17. What do you think the following scriptures are trying to tell us?
    a. Romans 12:1
    b. 1 Corinthians 12
    c. Ephesians 4

18. Have you ever completed a study on giftings? If yes, were your gifts the ones you thought they would be? If you never have, look in your local bookstore for one of the several books available to help you. Peter Wagner is one author who has a variety of simple studies, including *Your Spiritual Gifts Can Help Your Church Grow.*

19. After you discover and record your giftings, ask yourself, "What is my passion?" Your passion is what really excites you when you think about it. Is it working with seniors; teaching kids, youth or young adults; or is it serving the church and just doing what needs to be done?

20. The third step in this exercise is to outline your talents. What do you enjoy doing and what are you good at? Do not be afraid to be completely honest (it is not bragging), so write them all down. If you are good at something but do not really enjoy it, then put it at the bottom of the list or leave it off completely. You should not agree to fill a position just because there is a hole that needs to be filled and you know you are capable. For example, I know I can sing fairly well but do not enjoy being on the worship team. Why then would I agree to join the team?

21. Our gifts and talents need to fit our personality type. Are you someone who likes to make lists and gather all the details, or do you like to come up with the ideas and then turn the project over to someone else? Decide if you are introverted (preferring to be alone, behind the scenes or only with very small groups) or extroverted (the person who would rather be around people and really does not like spending large blocks of time by yourself). Once again, there are resources available in your local bookstore to help you. You can look for *Personality Plus* by Florence Littauer, or one by Myers-Briggs.

22. Finally, what are your life experiences? These can be from recent years or throughout your lifetime. Once you begin to write them down, you will realize that you have gone through many good and bad times, which can, in turn, help you to show empathy to others who are going through the same or similar times.

Memory Verse

"God made us what we are. In Christ Jesus, God made us to do good works, which God planned in advance for us to live our lives doing" (Ephesians 2:10 NCV).

Newfound Facts

_____

_____

_____

_____

_____

_____

❧ Therefore let it be known to you, brethren, that through this Man is preached to you the forgiveness of sins ❧

Acts 13:38

4

Unexpected Messenger

He used the divorced

(John 4:1-42)

The Woman at the Well was not automatically someone we would think God would use, but she became the centre of his plan for her town. We will never know her name, but Jesus knew, and it does not take long for us to discover how God was able to use her to reach so many others.

This woman had three strikes against her. First of all, the townspeople did not consider her a good woman because she had been married and divorced, not once, but five times, and was now living with a man who was not her husband. Second, she was a woman living in a man's world. Men considered women to be of much lower status. Plato actually felt that only men received souls when they were born, and it would be a man's poor fate to be reincarnated as a woman. He went on to say, "Obviously it is only men who are complete human beings and can hope for ultimate fulfillment; the best a woman can hope for is to become a man." Aristotle wrote, "Females are imperfect males accidentally produced by their father's inadequacy." Continuing, he maintains that women's inferiority lies in a defect. "Women are defective by nature" because they cannot reproduce semen, which contains a full human being. Another man in the first century once PRAYED, "Thank you Lord that you did not make me a slave, a gentile, or a woman." The final strike for this woman was that she was a Samaritan. The Samaritans were despised by the Jews.

The Woman at the Well was very aware of what people thought of her, and she was ashamed of the turns that her life had taken. She was so embarrassed that she would go in the heat of the day to get water just to avoid the other women and their ridicule, stares and finger-pointing. Nevertheless, Jesus saw something different in her, so he reached out to her.

When Jesus asked her for a drink of water, she was startled because he had no cup. Surely he would not want to drink from her container, for she was a Samaritan. The wall of rejection put up by the Jews toward Samaritans was all she could think of and all she could see.

Many of us have a tendency to put up our own walls as we focus on things that have happened that we cannot change. Hours are wasted asking ourselves, "Why did I do that? Why did I say that? Why did I even think that?" We cannot change any of the past, but we often cannot or do not seem to let it go. However, the person to whom we did something, said something or even about whom we thought something may never have known our true thoughts or feelings. We may not have forgotten—but they have.

When I was younger, much younger, I dated a very nice young man whom I really liked and who I knew really liked me. He asked me to his 12th grade graduation, functions with our friends and a formal banquet. I gladly went to all of them and completely enjoyed myself. One night, I decided I just did not want to date him anymore. Instead of telling him how I felt, I took the cowardly way out and showed up the next week with another fellow. In the following months, friends told me how much I had hurt him. Over the following years, I continued to feel very guilty, often thinking of how cruel I had been, but I had also built up a wall to try to push away everyone connected with the situation. Ten years later, at a group reunion, I knew in my heart that I needed to apologize and ask his forgiveness even though so many years had passed. To my delight, he did not even remember the incident, but said he forgave me, and for the rest of the evening we had a great time with other longtime friends.

We build up walls to prevent others from getting too close to us because we feel uncomfortable or ashamed of what may have transpired between us. We feel that they are *our* walls and hurts and we just cannot or will not let them go. When we do this, we rob ourselves of true and fulfilling relationships. It is the same in our relationship with God; we put walls up because we know that we have asked him to forgive us so many times for the same thing. We decide that we cannot possibly come back again, consequently robbing ourselves of the favour and mercy that God desires to pour out onto us.

The Woman at the Well must have felt some of that self-condemnation. She was embarrassed because she did not have her life together according to her society's standards; therefore, she avoided the townspeople because of their attitude toward her.

Jesus can see through our walls just as he saw through hers. He asked her for a drink and was willing to accept it from her and even go beyond that and drink from her container. I am certain that she must have wondered what this man was talking about when he not only asked for a drink of water to quench his thirst but also offered her water that would quench her thirst forever. He spoke, not just of the water we drink, but of much more—"living water" (John 4:10 NKJV).

As they conversed, Jesus asked this woman many questions, which she answered openly and honestly, sometimes returning questions of her own. She was a feisty woman, pushing Jesus to explain details that she did not understand and wanted to know. For example, when she wondered about the living water, she asked, "Are you greater than our father Jacob who gave us this well and drank from it himself, as well as his sons and his livestock?" (John 4:12 NKJV). She was not going to take everything he said as truth without him explaining it further. She was not about to be completely attentive until she realized that there was something very different about this man.

Knowing that it was not proper for a woman to speak to a man, especially a stranger, without her husband present, Jesus followed the rules of the times and asked her to go and get her husband. When she answered that she had no husband, he said he knew that and then continued to give an account of her life's history. How did he know? He was a stranger; yet he knew so much of her life story. Who was this person?

Prior to this encounter, Jesus had never actually said that he WAS the Messiah, but would tell people that he was the "Son of Man." Yet, with this woman, it was different. This was the first time that Jesus confirmed that he really was the Messiah, the Christ. Hearing this, she became so excited that she ran to the town to tell everyone to come and see this man. Could he be the Messiah, given that he knew everything about her?

Why would the people in town ever listen to her? The women despised her and the men, I am sure, did not think much of her either. Yet, they saw something different in this despised woman, something they had never seen before. Could it be the fact that she was running wildly into town, probably yelling and looking like she had just lost her mind? No, it was her face—it was glowing. Seeing this, the men went to the well to see for themselves who this man really was. Her excitement was so extreme that she ran away and left her water jug behind, beside Jesus. Could he possibly be the One?

Salvation came to many people that day because Jesus was able to work through this unsuspecting woman. This single incident shows that God cares so much for us that he will look past our culture, our gender, our age and yes, even our background. Think of it—is this the woman you would pick to share such an important message? She may have felt that she was simply at the well at the wrong time. However, it was the perfect time and the perfect situation, and there was no one better for Jesus to use to get in touch with so many lives.

Sometimes we avoid discussions about Jesus because we think others may know more than we do or we are afraid of looking foolish if they ask a question and we do not know the answer. When we shirk those opportunities, we may be robbing both others and ourselves of an encounter with the true living water. Think about the ramifications if the woman had not continued to ask Jesus questions about the living water of which he was speaking. An entire town might have lost the opportunity to hear the Word of God from Jesus himself. Do not worry about looking foolish or uneducated; life is a time of learning. I once heard a quote that said, "When you stop learning, you die." Do you want to keep learning? I know I do.

Turn Your Heart

Jesus is waiting for you and me to come to him and talk with him just like this woman did.

What would you ask Jesus if he were sitting beside you today? Take your questions and write them down in your journal. When you receive your answers, write them down too.

Remember the scripture that says "And whatever we ask we receive from Him, because we keep His commandments and do those things that are pleasing in His sight" (1 John 3:22 NKJV). If a child never asked any questions, how would she ever learn? God is willing to listen to all of our rants, ravings, questions and yes, even our attitudes; but then it is his turn to speak and our turn to listen. He is waiting to reveal what he wants to do in our lives and what he wants us to do for him. Just as the Woman at the Well had the choice to accept the living water, we have the choice to listen to him and follow his will.

When Jesus acknowledged the fact that he really knew the woman for everything she was, he let her know that through it all he was still willing to accept her right then and there. He knew that she was a sinner but he saw beyond that—he saw her as a person who was very important to the kingdom and as the child of God that she was. If he had not done that, she probably would have kept her wall up, trying to hide her past, her shame and her sin from God, thinking that she was not worthy. God knows our sin anyway, so let's stop wasting time; admit it and ask for forgiveness. Someone once said, "When you forgive another, you release a prisoner and the prisoner is often yourself."

What walls have you built up? Are you ready to release them? Today, right where you are, turn them over to Jesus and let him help to tear them down. He is ready as soon as you let him in.

Let's Pray

Jesus, you already know everything about me before I even come to you, but still you accept me just as I am. I thank you that you love me too much to leave me like I am today and you pour out your grace and mercy on my life. I thank you that I can confidently bring all of my questions to you, and I know that in your time you will reveal the answers. God, there are so many things that I just do not understand, and I pray for your peace and your help to understand them. Help me to be patient, allowing you to work in me and through me. I ask you to help me tear down the walls that keep me from the fullness of your love and your plan for my life. Help me to see others as you would see them. Give me a new boldness to reach out to the unsaved of this world so that they may come to know you as the true living water that you are. Help me to become the person that you desire me to be. Use me, Lord.

Future Study Scriptures

- Exodus 15:2
- Job 13:16
- Romans10:10
- 1 Thessalonians 5:9
- Hebrews 5:9
- 2 Samuel 22:36
- Psalm3:8
- Ephesians 6:17
- Titus 2:11

Additional Analysis

For further investigation, read John 4:1-42

1. We are never told the name of the Woman at the Well. Why do you think that is?

2. Even though we may not be able to call her by name, how well do you think the Lord knew her? (Also read Psalm 139:13-16 and Jeremiah 1:5.)

3. We learned that she went to the well in the heat of the day to avoid the other women in the town because of their treatment of her. Think of a time when you received unfair treatment or when so-called friends or the people of the church judged you unfairly. How did you handle it? Did you leave and avoid them? Did you confront them with their misinformation?

4. Luke 6:37 tells us what to do instead of judging others. In your own words, rewrite this scripture as it pertains to you right now.

5. When we get into situations in which we do not feel comfortable, we build up walls. What are some of the ways in which you have built up walls? How can you tear them down?

6. Has there ever been a time in your life when you thought you were in the wrong place at the wrong time and it turned out to be the perfect place at the perfect time? Elaborate.

7. Scripture tells us that this woman left her water jug behind when she went to tell the townspeople what had just happened. What do you think is the significance of her leaving it rather than carrying it with her?

8. Knowing the way the townspeople treated this woman, why do you think she even bothered to tell them about Jesus, let alone rushing to tell them?

9. What lessons have you learned from her life and her conversation with Jesus?

10. Describe this story as it would be told in the 21st century.

Memory Verse

"You have the gifts that the Holy One gave you, so you all know the truth" (1 John 2:20 NCV).

Newfound Facts

_____

_____

_____

_____

_____

_____

_____

_____

_____

_____

_____

_____

_____

_____

_____

_____

_____
_____
_____
_____
_____
_____
_____
_____
_____
_____
_____
_____
_____
_____
_____
_____
_____
_____
_____
_____

So teach us to number our days that we may gain a heart of wisdom.

Psalm 90:12

5

A Wise Peacemaker

He used the married

(1 Samuel 25)

Abigail was a very wise woman and a peacemaker whom God was able to use to save numerous lives. In addition, she was quick-witted, decisive, a hard worker and the wife of a very rich shepherd. She had it made: "she was a woman of good understanding and beautiful appearance" 1 Samuel 25:3 (NKJV).

There was just one major problem—her husband. Nabal was arrogant and stubborn; he always had to be right. The end of 1 Samuel 25:3 says, "but the man was harsh and evil in his doings." He should have taken wisdom lessons from Abigail, but maybe he did not because his name, *Nabal*, actually means "fool."

A modern-day description of Abigail and Nabal can be found in the story of a couple who got lost while on vacation. They ended up in a huge argument because the husband was too stubborn to stop and ask for directions; he just kept telling his wife that he knew exactly where he was going. After driving for several hours, neither of them speaking to the other, they passed a mule in a field. The husband looked at his wife and asked, "Is that a relative of yours?"

To which she quickly answered, "Yes, by marriage."

David and his men had been working to protect the area, including the hills where Nabal kept his sheep, thereby protecting Nabal's livelihood. Nabal and his men had 3,000 sheep to shear, yet they managed to take the time to have a great party with an abundance of food and drink. At the exact same time as the feast, David sent 10 of his men to Nabal to request some provisions. Nabal was definitely in David's debt, but that did not seem to matter to him, since he turned David's men away with nothing, practically spitting on them. Nabal really was a fool! He had just insulted not only the very people who had been protecting his livelihood, but also one of the world's most powerful men at that time. David became enraged and began to plot his revenge. Had it not been for the quick thinking of Abigail, David and his men would have carried out their plan to kill Nabal and every other male in the area.

We all know people who have a bad habit of speaking first and thinking later. My grandmother had a favourite phrase, "The easiest words to take back in the morning are those that are left unsaid." I think Nabal should have heeded that advice, kept his mouth shut and let someone give David the food he requested. This was not the first time that Abigail had to save her husband from his own foolishness, but this time there was a soon-to-be king involved.

If this incident occurred today, I can only imagine what the scene might be like as she returned home. She would probably wait until the next morning when Nabal was suffering from yet another major hangover after eating and drinking with the boys all night. "Well, Nabal, you have done it again! Once again I have had to bail you out! When are you going to learn to have some brains?" On and on and on she might go, since her disgust would replace any respect and obedience she felt toward her husband. After all, this woman was living with a fool and she had to use her wisdom to bail him out time after time.

Abigail was not only quick-thinking; she was also very wise and politically correct. Before she went to see David, she gathered food and drink for him and his men. When she met him, she truly humbled herself by falling to the ground on her face before him. I cannot imagine how frightening it must have been since he could have given the order to kill her in a second—but still she went. She was one woman meeting with

David and hundreds of his men; still, she knew that, at the very least, she had to go and try to salvage this situation. She had to courageously face the fact that, from being on the road for so long, these men would make a sports arena locker room smell sweet, not to mention that they were furious and on the warpath for her husband and the other men with him.

She started speaking to David by acknowledging the fact that he was angry with Nabal. She told David that Nabal was a fool, that even his name meant fool and that foolishness followed him wherever he went. She continued her appeal and asked that David remove his anger from Nabal and divert it to her. Was she crazy? Why should she take the blame for something that she'd had absolutely no part in actually deciding? David could have called for her life to end at that very moment. Yet, she went on speaking and acknowledged that she had not seen his men when they'd arrived, implying that she would have given them food and drink immediately. She was smart. If David was going to soften his heart toward her, this would be the beginning. David now had the food, he had an apology and he had her acknowledgement that her husband, Nabal, was just plain stupid.

Continuing, but using very carefully chosen words, she started to remind David that vengeance should be from God rather than from him. That must have hurt. Have you ever been so angry with someone that you wanted to see him or her as unhappy as you were at that moment? Revenge is not sweet and consequences need to come from God, not from us. We have to release our hurt and anger to God and let him do his work.

Abigail was really on a roll. She brought up how God can hurl the lives of our enemies from the sling. Oh, there it is—that image of a sling and memories of killing Goliath are now racing back to David. This woman is good! She has his attention; she has brought up God, the sling and Goliath—what will be next?

She went on to remind David that God would deal with Nabal for not taking care of him and his men. She told David that if he carried out his plan for Nabal and the other men, then it would be no different from the way in which Saul was treating David. Abigail continued, saying that it would be a politically incorrect move for David because, when he became king, he would be starting his reign with enemies from Nabal's tribe, the tribe of Israel. Not only had she now saved the life of her poor and pathetic husband, she had also saved that of every other male in his tribe, and saved all of the women from becoming widows and the children from becoming fatherless. She prevented David from committing a sin against God by taking on the reprimand for Nabal that God himself intended. God's judgment came quickly; 10 days after receiving the news of Abigail's actions, Nabal died.

The death of Nabal would normally have been a genuine tragedy for Abigail, but the story does not end there. God had a plan for her, as he does for each of us, and soon she would receive the blessing of her work. David's experience with Abigail gave him enormous respect for her. He saw that she was a woman of great wisdom, compassion and sensitivity. When David heard about the death of Nabal, he sent word for Abigail to come to him, and he took her as his own bride.

When situations come upon us unexpectedly, it may be hard not to panic or run, but we need to remember that God is not far away. We need to stop, take a deep breath and use the intelligence that God has given us to handle the problem. Just as God gave Abigail special abilities, he gives us abilities upon which we need to draw. Abigail quickly discovered that if her husband was going to continually put her into difficult situations, she would have to think fast and act quickly and decisively to calm one storm after another. She was able to prove herself very capable. She earned God's favour and David's respect.

Turn Your Heart

God wants us to pray for our husbands. We need to lift them up and work toward becoming a team. We need to be ready to serve God together, not like Abigail and Nabal. They were not just opposites—they were off-the-charts different! One was generous, loving and wise, while the other was generally bigheaded and stingy. Nabal was also a complete fool, never thinking before he spoke or acted.

Pray for wisdom in your marriage and in your family.

Ask God to grow your relationship with your spouse, special friend or other loved ones. We need to give up the desire to control them; they are not remote-controlled cars that we can send out and bring back whenever we want to.

Ask God to reveal any bitterness, hurt or resentment you have concerning your spouse, then confess it and really give it to God, releasing it once and for all. As you release it, ask God to fill the void with good emotions of love, tenderness, caring and forgiveness.

Let's Pray

God, I release to you any negative feelings I have right now. I ask you, Father, to take over and be the head of this home and all my relationships. I ask you to direct us to the work that you would have us do together. Lord, I pray for my husband in every area of his life—his health, his work, his relationships with those with whom he works, his family, his church and, above all, with you. Let nothing stop the work and the passion that you have placed in his life. Help me to be an asset, not a hindrance to him. Lord, I give you any unforgiveness or bitterness that I have for him or others with whom I am in a relationship and ask you to replace it with good in my heart. I pray for other family members and friends with whom you have put me in relationships and ask for my husband and me to work as one so that all tasks can be done cohesively and for you. Help my husband and me to keep you as the centre of everything we do. Help us to see any other strongholds that are keeping us back from your fullness, and Lord, I ask for your help in releasing them to you RIGHT NOW!

Future Study Scriptures

- Exodus 31:3
- Exodus 35:26
- Deuteronomy 4:6
- 1 Kings 4:30
- Proverbs 2:2
- Proverbs 12:8
- Ecclesiastes 2:13
- Ecclesiastes 9:18

📖 Job 12:13   📖 Jeremiah 8:9
📖 Psalm 90:12   📖 Matthew 5:9
📖 Psalm 111:10   📖 Revelation 7:12

Additional Analysis

For further investigation, read: 1 Samuel 25

1. Is there one or more of Abigail's characteristics in this story that relate to you? If so, which ones and why?

2. A person's words can teach us a lot about him or her. What do you think the words of Nabal, David and Abigail say about them? What do your words to others say about you?

3. Abigail and Nabal seem completely incompatible as a couple. How do women today respond when they find themselves married to men like Nabal? If different from your answer above, how do you think they should handle it?

4. From everything that we have read about the relationship between David and Nabal, do you think David's request to Nabal for provisions for himself and his men was realistic?

5. David snapped a response to Nabal that was reactionary rather than necessarily correct. What does Luke 6:27-31 say that we are to do when someone treats us unfairly?

6. Looking at the actions of Nabal, David and Abigail, can you think of times when you have acted like each of them? Can you describe them?

7. Thinking back to my grandmother's favourite phrase, "The easiest words to take back in the morning are those that are left unsaid," are there times when this statement does not apply?

8. When Abigail went to David, she demonstrated great resourcefulness but also faced great danger. What risks do you think she took in approaching David and his men?

9. Abigail knew the words to use to get under David's skin. What were those statements and why do you think they influenced David so much?

10. How do you react when you discover that someone has shown poor judgment in his or her choices? What do we need to do if his or her choices affect us directly?

11. There is a fine line between meddling and helping. At what point do you think it is good to step in and speak out on behalf of others?

12. Who did Abigail help by her actions?

Memory Verse

"But if any of you need wisdom you should ask God for it. He is generous with wisdom and will not criticize you for it" (James 1:5 NCV).

Newfound Facts

_____

_____

_____

_____

_____

_____

❧ And now, Lord, what do I wait for? My hope is in You. ❧

Psalm 39:7

6

Trust and Obedience—Twice Over

He used the widows

(1Kings 17:8-24, Mark 12:40-42)

Have you ever looked at a situation and immediately thought that it was completely hopeless and dark? The deeper you looked, all you saw was blackness, with not even a small trickle of light squeaking through? Such a situation seems impossible; in fact, it appears so bleak that you wonder if even God can fix this one.

The widow of Zarephath must have had similar thoughts. She was a widow with a young son, and she had no money left. Not only did she have no income, she was also living in a land suffering from a severe drought. Her cupboards had only enough food left for one more meal, and she could not go to her neighbours because no one else in the land was doing very well either. She felt utterly and completely alone. What else could she do but make one last meal for her and her son and then sit and wait to die? To her, the situation could not have seemed much darker or more hopeless.

As she was out picking up sticks to make a fire to prepare the last loaf of bread, a man came and asked for a drink of water. Could he not see that she was busy? Who was this man anyway? Did he not know that she was weak and ready to give up? He wanted a drink. Okay, being the gracious woman that she was, she went to get him a drink, only to have him call after her to bring him some bread too. Bread?! She only had enough flour and oil for her little son and herself for that one final meal! If she gave it to him, they would have even less. She turned back to him to tell him her situation, but the guest would not leave it there. Elijah spoke back, giving her a word from God that "the bin of flour shall not be used up nor shall the jar of oil run dry until the day the Lord sends rain on the earth" 1 Kings 17:14 (NKJV).

Now she had a decision to make, would she believe Elijah and have faith in the God of her fathers, or would she think of herself and her son? It was more than she could ever envision: God was going to do a miracle in her heart and her life as well as in her kitchen. Even so, she obeyed. We can only imagine her excitement when the containers really did not run out of flour or oil. Day after day, she would continue to bake the amount of bread she would need for that day. Although the jars may not have been full, there was not a day that they were empty.

This alone could have been the happy conclusion to what was, at first, a tragic story; but the story of this little widow does not end there. Her only son, who was to be her sole caregiver for the rest of her life, became ill and died. Like her husband, her son was now gone and she really was alone—very alone. She had trusted God the first time and believed his prophet when he had said that she would not hunger, but this time her son was *dead*. There was no heartbeat, no blood pressure and no movement—nothing except a cold, stiff body. She accused God and Elijah of turning their backs on her and leaving her alone with no hope. Now she would surely die.

I remember the day that my brother found his baby lifeless in his crib and had to call my parents with the news. An incredible feeling of helplessness and grief overcame our entire family. I can still remember my mother's cries when she heard the news, asking God why he would take such a young child who had not had an opportunity to live and grow up. The feeling of disbelief, thinking he could not be gone, was overwhelming; after all, we had not even seen him yet.

The mother who listened to Elijah had experienced God as he provided when she was hungry, and she would now have to trust again. She had to believe that God could send life back into her son, but that would be a stretch for even the most trusting individual. Immediately, as Elijah prayed, renewal and restoration did come upon the young man. Try to imagine her excitement when her son stood up strong and healthy again! What a witness for God she must have become.

Just as God loved this woman too much to leave her where she was—in her pit of despair—he loved my brother too much to leave him and his wife in their grief. They soon discovered that there was another child on the way—a child not to replace the one they had lost, but to help replace some of the extreme sadness with joy. For this widow, God demonstrated his great miracles of provision and life, making her a witness to his magnificent mercy and love. God was stretching her faith as he sometimes stretches ours. Did this woman, who remained nameless, do mighty things? We are never told, but it is easy to imagine her telling her neighbours and friends all about how God had helped her. Her faith went from a mustard seed to a giant plant because of God's work and grace in her family.

There is a story in the Bible of another widow about whom many of us will have heard at one time or another. Just like the previous woman, the story never reveals her name; she is simply referred to as a very poor widow. She entered the temple, hand in her pocket, perhaps rolling the two coins around her fingers as they rattled against one another. These coins were all that remained from her husband who had died, and giving them away now would leave her completely destitute. Should she give them to the Lord and trust that he would provide for her needs, or should she use these coins to try to feed herself one final time?

I have met people whose lives exemplify this story. For instance, once a young girl was helping count the Sunday offering. After emptying an envelope filled with only pennies, the second counter casually, but a little sarcastically, asked, "Who would ever put in all these pennies?" His disgust arose from the fact that now he would have to count them and it might take a few extra minutes. She looked at him with a tear in her eye and said, "I did. It was all I had." We may never know when someone has given all that he or she has, but we do know that God can work miracles with those few pennies. We also know that God values these gifts as much as larger ones—maybe even more—because they are, without doubt, gifts of love and true sacrifice.

This widow gave her last few coins, thinking that no one would notice, but Jesus did. Maybe on earth men did not see, but such was not the case in heaven, because, at that moment, a place of honour was prepared for her. She may not have felt that she was capable of doing much, but she did as much as she could with the little that she had. She took a step of extraordinary faith and trust in God. She came with a little and went home with a strong hope and belief that God would take care of and provide for her.

How easy it would have been for this woman to deem two coins incapable of doing any good and decide that she might as well keep them. This story proves that it does not matter the size of the gift, but rather, the attitude of the giver. She really gave until it hurt, not only giving her last two pennies, but literally giving everything she had—her money, her trust, her future and her heart. She laid everything before God, said it was now his to deal with, and she left, trusting that he would take care of her.

For us today, this story is a wonderful reminder that whatever we give is important to God as well as to our own personal contentment. After reading this, a friend reminded me that not only monetary giving comes into play in this story. Many people have some form of physical immobility. Maybe they cannot come out and help us to carry lumber for that building project or go out on campaign to reach people for Jesus, but they are willing to do the jobs that many feel are insignificant. They can fold brochures or make phone calls to confirm volunteers for the projects and many other things that help the front and centre people to accomplish their jobs more efficiently. Society has a tendency to look only at those who are working at the forefront, but God sees everyone and cares about what is really in the heart and attitude of the giver.

God worked through these two women, presenting them to us as a demonstration of faith and trust in him. We have no idea how many other people they touched as they retold their stories or how many they reach out to today as we read their stories in the Word. We do not always have to give hundreds or thousands of dollars, but we need to trust God and know that what he places on our hearts is what we are to give. It may be money, it may be time or it may be ourselves. Remember, if you ignore promptings from the Holy Spirit on giving a gift or offering, you are cheating yourself out of a blessing and you are cheating God.

Both of these women gave of themselves and what they had—the first, her food, and the second, her money. Are you feeling a challenge to give today? Maybe it is to be a sponsor to a child through one of the television programs or your church. It might be to take time to visit seniors in nursing homes. Maybe your challenge is for you to drive your neighbour to the doctor, to get groceries or to church on Sunday. Whatever it is, be obedient and give with a willing heart.

God wants to bless us but he wants us to be obedient to the promptings of the Holy Spirit. We can easily miss the simplest opportunities to bless God's people. I can remember once, when I was travelling, I went into a service station to pay for my gas. In front of me was a trucker who was trying to purchase food for his trip. He tried to use his debit card, only to have it rejected for lack of funds. When he tried swiping a second card, he got the same response. He turned and left, leaving the food he wanted on the counter. The entire time I felt like I should offer to pay his bill for him. After all, it was only a few dollars, but I just stood there and waited my turn to pay for my own purchase. To this day, I think about this man and realize I missed an opportunity to bless him with the love of Jesus in addition to missing the blessing for myself.

We need to lean on God and trust that he is there to take care of us, even if that means raising someone from the grips of death.

Turn Your Heart

God wants us to turn to him and give it ALL to him to deal with. Are we giving him our tithes and offerings, our talents, our time, our families and our futures, or are we holding back? We often have a tendency to give our families and problems to God, laying them at his feet, but just as he goes to get them, we grab them back. How would you feel if someone gave you a gift and just as you were about to take it from her, she grabbed it back and yelled "Just Kidding!"?

What is it that you are holding back from God today? Write down the areas that you need to give to God, and then pray that he will help you to release them for good.

Is there room in your heart to trust him more, believe in him more and rely on him more? He wants you to become a witness to others, just like these two women were witnesses to those around them. Just as we prayed in the last chapter, we need to seek out that new boldness for him. God loves you just as he loved these two women and went to great lengths to prove his love for them. He will do the same for you.

Let's Pray

God, help me to release to you the things that I keep holding onto so very tightly. As you did with the widow, fill my containers with a never-ending supply of flour and oil. Help me, Lord, to trust you in times of crisis and not just in the good times when it is easy. Even though I often lose sight of you, the deliverer, during the dilemma, I thank you that you do not lose sight of me. You continually draw me back into your loving arms. I thank you, Lord, for what you are doing in my life and in the lives of those around me.

I ask you, Lord, to help me leave situations with you and not tell you how to fix them, but rather trust you to do it according to your plan, not mine. I ask you, Lord, to help me to become a woman you can use who trusts you, has faith in you and allows you to work in and through her. Help me, God, to be sensitive to the promptings of your Holy Spirit and to use wisdom and discernment in those times. Help me to understand completely when it is you calling on me and not something else. I love you, Lord, and want to be your willing servant, not offering you gifts just to grab them back. You gave the ultimate gift of your son for me so that I may live free and able.

Future Study Scriptures

- 2 Samuel 22:3
- 1 Chronicles5:20
- Job 13:15
- Psalm 4:5
- Psalm 5:11
- Psalm 16:1
- Psalm 18:2
- Proverbs 3:5
- Proverbs 16:20
- Isaiah 12:2
- Jeremiah 17:17
- Nahum 1:7
- Mark 10:24
- 2 Corinthians 1:10
- 1 Ephesians 1:13

Additional Analysis

For further investigation, read 1Kings 17; 10-24, Mark 12:40-42

1. Why do you think God had Elijah ask this widow for bread even though he knew how very desperate she was?

2. This woman knew very well that she might be preparing her last meal, so why did she say yes to this man's request for food?

3. Have you ever had a time when you felt that you really needed to do something but you did not know why or how to do it? Explain.

4. Has God ever surprised you with something that you absolutely were not expecting, as he did with this woman when he filled the jars with oil and flour? Try to elaborate.

5. In addition to the grief of losing her son, what emotions do you think this woman experienced after her son died? Do you think she felt abandoned and let down? Do you think she felt lost and alone?

6. She was looking to place blame on someone or something for her new situation. On whom or what did she place it—on God, Elijah or perhaps her sins?

7. Was there a time when the stretching of your faith got to a point where you did not think you would be able to carry on? If you can, describe it. What was the outcome?

8. Do you see ways in which you can practise your faith today, even if you do not feel stretched?

9. Do you believe that stretching is how we grow in Christ and that without it we can stagnate and start to take things for granted?

10. When tested a second time, as happened to this lady, do you think people have a tendency to forget the miracles of the past? Why do you think their faith wavers?

11. For the second time, this woman saw God move radically on her behalf. What was the reaction of the widow when her son was returned to her? What do you think happened to her faith?

12. The second widow gave two coins in the offering. Why were those coins so significant?

13. Why was Jesus even watching what people were putting into the offering?

14. If you were there that day, what would he say to you about your offering and the attitude with which you gave it?

15. What does the Word say about giving from the heart?

16. Why did Jesus see a greater value in this woman's gift compared to some of the larger ones?

17. What guidelines concerning giving appear in the following scriptures?
    a. Exodus 25:2
    b. 1 Chronicles 29:14
    c. Matthew 6:2-4
    d. 1 Corinthians 16:2
    e. 2 Corinthians 9:6-7

18. Sometimes the Holy Spirit will place it on our hearts to give, but we question it and fight with him about it. Has this ever happened to you? What do you think is the result if we ignore the promptings and give excuses for why we cannot?

19. What do the examples of these two women say to you?

Memory Verse

"Be alert. Continue strong in the faith. Have courage and be strong" (1 Corinthians 16:13 NCV).

Newfound Facts

_____

_____

_____

_____

_____

_____

_____

_____

_____

_____

_____

_____

_____

_____

_____

_____

_____

_____

_____

_____

_____

_____

_____

_____

_____

_____

_____

_____

❧ Then Jesus answered and said to her, "O woman, great is your faith! Let it be to you as you desire." And her daughter was healed from that very hour. ❧

Matthew 15:28

7

Determination

He used the mother

(Matthew 15:21-28)

Jesus and his disciples had just gone into the region of Tyre and Sidon to pray and rest. Sharing the message of God and being surrounded by people every hour of the day had completely consumed them emotionally and physically. Now what they all needed was to get away from the crowds and the noise in order to have an opportunity to be alone and to allow their bodies to receive physical and emotional refreshment.

This area should have been the perfect location because it was inhabited by pagans, unbelievers and people who worshipped several false gods rather than people eager to follow Jesus. However, this land was also home to one very desperate mother. Her daughter was suffering terribly from demon possession, and this mother was willing to go to any length to try to find a cure for her child. She must have endured great hardship while helplessly watching her only daughter, not knowing what the demons controlling her would have her do next. Moreover, the townspeople isolated them both because no one wanted to get too close to her daughter for fear of what she might do. How terribly alone and afraid for her daughter and herself this woman must have felt.

How thrilled this Canaanite woman must have been when she discovered that Jesus and his followers were in her town! She had heard what this man was doing for the Jews and wondered if he might also do it for her daughter. Could he really do it? Would he do it? When she got close to him, she began calling out, "Lord, Son of David, have mercy on me!" We can assume that her petition must have been continuous, because the disciples pleaded with Jesus to send her away. However, Jesus did not even acknowledge her.

This mother's level of protection for her child was like that of a mother lion; she would do anything to save her young, and she was going to make this man answer her and help her. She remained very persistent with her plea, "Lord, Son of David, have mercy on me!" each time increasing her intensity. The more Jesus ignored her, the louder she became until she was almost hysterical. She finally got so loud and frantic that the disciples must have wondered if the demon had entered her as well.

Could she have been a believer in this land of pagans, or was she using this situation strictly for her benefit? I think that even though she may have struggled with questions about the reality of this man, she must have believed. If not, you would think that when he ignored her after she called out a few times, she would have left in anger and disappointment. She would have concluded that he was not all that she had heard him being made out to be. He must be a fake.

Why, though, would Jesus ignore her? Was it because he was tired and thought she would go away? Was it because she was a woman? We have already read that women were poorly thought of by most men of those days. For this woman to risk even approaching Jesus required enormous courage because women did not make the first step to speak to men. Jesus already had a reputation for demonstrating compassion to people, including women and, above all, widows, so this cannot be the reason.

Was it to see how the disciples would react? They were tired and showed their anger and frustration as they begged Jesus to get rid of her quickly. Maybe they thought that if Jesus gave her what she wanted, she would leave and give them the rest and peace that they were so desperately seeking.

Was it to see if she really did have faith? It might have been, because we do know that she showed a great measure of faith and determination in her approach.

This woman had to make a decision—would she continue trying to get this man to pay attention to her, or would she just walk away and give up? She chose to be faith-driven and even more determined, falling to her knees in worship in front of him. This woman was not going to take "no" for an answer. She knew in her heart that if anyone could heal her daughter it would be this man, Jesus, and she was not going to go away or give up until he did. She needed to have him at the very least *try* to cure her daughter.

When Jesus finally answered her, he told her that he did not come to earth for her people but for the Jews, and that he should not be taking away from them to give to her. What a blow that must have been for her, especially when he went on to describe it as feeding the dog at the expense of his own chosen children. Matthew 15:26 tells it all, "But He answered and said, 'It is not good to take the children's bread and throw it to the little dogs'" (NKJV).

The stinging rebuke in Jesus' response would have stopped most people in their tracks—but not this woman, not this mother. The hair on the back of her neck stood up and she pushed her shoulders back, looked him right in the eye and, with even greater passion, came back with, "Yes, Lord, yet even the dogs eat the crumbs that fall from their Master's table" Matthew 15:27(NKJV).

When our granddaughter was learning to feed herself and no longer wanted her food, she would drop or throw it onto the floor, and the dog quickly learned that there would be scraps for him to devour if he only hung around long enough. This mother knew that Jesus could do what she was asking, and her faith in him was undaunted. She was going to continue to pester him until she got what she wanted. After all, this was not just for her, but for her daughter.

We still have to wonder why Jesus would treat her like this. This is not like the Jesus about whom we teach. The Jesus we know is loving and caring and will do anything for people, but this person sounds downright mean and rude. Even though Jesus saw her faith, maybe he was testing that faith. This woman now had an opportunity to put her faith into action. Jesus saw her tenacity and humility, and he later referred to her as having "great faith" (Matthew15:28 NIV), a term that he did not often use.

Do you ever feel like God is testing your faith? There are times when we pray and pray for something that we know is right, but we hear or see no answer and start to wonder if God is even listening. We wonder if he even cares, because why else would he ignore us?

When I first became a believer, a woman shared with me how she had prayed for her husband for 25 years before he finally accepted Jesus into his heart. I thought to myself that my story would be different; 25 years seemed excessively long. It has now been 25 plus years of praying for my husband and I still know that it will happen, even though only God knows when.

There are times that I believe God seems to ignore us because what we are asking for is just plain wrong or the timing isn't right. If your child comes to you and asks for the hammer because his brother is driving him crazy and he is going to drive him a good one, are you going to let your child have the hammer? No, because you know that it is not good for either child. God is the same; sometimes our requests are so bizarre that he is silent out of love. Is that not why we pray, "not MY will but YOUR will be done on earth as it is in heaven"?

The Canaanite woman's request was in the best interest of her child, so why did Jesus not answer it immediately? It was not harmful or selfish—it was good. Jesus had not refused to heal anyone else about whom we read. He had healed the blind, the lame and even the dead.

In situations like this, we need to ask ourselves: "Do I really trust God to do it? Do I really believe he can do it? What is my attitude in asking?" Ouch! Now it all comes back to my attitude. I can ask and ask, but in my heart do I really trust, or do I think that God owes me this one? Can he not see how good I have been and how long I have been asking? He must know I trust him, because otherwise I would just quit asking! But there is that "he owes me" attitude again. Patsy Clairmont refers to it as "sportin' a 'tude."

What "tude" are you sporting today? Is it our fault that God does not answer all of our prayers—even when we think they are good? No, but we need to ask God to work in our hearts to help us to check our attitude and to see if it may be harmful or not in his plan concerning the matter in question.

The Canaanite mother showed her trust and faith in Jesus through her persistence and determination to help her daughter. Jesus rewarded her by giving her daughter back to her for them to develop a new and healthy relationship. How did she keep her faith and trust in Jesus even though he was giving her the great brush-off? She had heard about this Jesus from the Jewish people and she chose to believe that he was the one person who could rescue her from her sins. She did not know why, but she did know that she could (she had to!) trust in him. She had heard of the work that he had done for others and knew that he would do it for her, too, if she only believed in him. She chose to trust in him and be like a little child who, when you say "no," comes back with "Please, please, please?" Children do not give up; neither did this woman and neither should we.

Can you imagine what kind of witness she became for Jesus after this event? She would not have needed to say a word, even though I am sure she did. All the townspeople had to do was look at her daughter to discover the difference. The one that they had ostracized for so long was now a normal, happy young girl just like any other. Her mom would have been so excited that she probably shared with everyone who would listen to the news of how this man named Jesus, the Son of David, had healed her daughter. God was able to use her because of her faith and trust in him, as well as her overwhelming perseverance.

Turn Your Heart

According to *Webster's Dictionary,* faith is "something that is believed especially with strong conviction," and the *Encarta Dictionary* describes it as "loyalty or allegiance to somebody or something with a strongly held set of beliefs or principles." Both of these descriptions equally convey faith as an extremely powerful word. Many of us say that we have an unbreakable faith in God, but how do we react when it is tested?

During a trial, how much do we really trust God to know and to do what is best for us? Faith can change things; it can move mountains and it can turn a "no" into a "yes."

1 Corinthians 16:13 says, "Watch, stand fast in the faith, be brave, be strong" (NKJV).

Max Lucado says that the story of the Canaanite woman does not portray a contemptuous God, but a willing one who delights in a sincere seeker. As mothers, we never want to see our children hurt or suffering. As mothers, our prayers play a vital part in our children's spiritual lives. We can never give up, no matter how old they are or whether or not they are living for Jesus at this moment. We must constantly pray for them.

3 John1: 3-4 tells us "It gave me great joy to have some brothers come and tell about your faithfulness to the truth and how you continue to walk in the truth. I have no greater joy than to hear that my children are walking in the truth" (NCV).

Think about the things you have been asking God for and then write them down. Now really give them up to God. Ask him to send the Holy Spirit to guide you and enable you to discern if you have the right attitude in asking the questions. Is your requests right for this time? Are you a sincere seeker concerning them?

Do not give up. We do not know the perfect timing of God, so trust him to work out his plan and manifest it in your life and the lives of your loved ones. Remember that God has our best interests at heart, just like a good parent would never do anything intentionally to hurt his or her child.

Let's Pray

God, this woman had a tenacity that would not allow her to give up. She may not have known who you really were, but she had heard of you and that was enough. She heard that you could heal her daughter if you chose to, and she would have done anything to see that happen. She trusted in you and I need to have that same kind of trust and faith. Help me, Lord, to have the kind of faith that, when we meet, you will say, "Daughter, you have shown great faith."

God, help my children and those around me to see Jesus living through and in me. My faith can grow, but only with the help and guidance that I can find by spending time in your Word and waiting on you. Help me, Lord, to realize that when you don't answer my prayers in the way that I think they should be answered, it is really in my best interest or there is a reason I do not need to really understand yet. You may say, "Not now," and I have to be patient, remembering that my timing is not always your timing. You have a great plan for my life and all things will work together for good for those who love and trust you.

Future Study Scriptures

- 📖 Judges 13:8
- 📖 1 Kings 17:23
- 📖 2 Kings 5:14
- 📖 Isaiah 58:8
- 📖 Malachi 4:2
- 📖 Matthew 1:23
- 📖 Matthew 4:23
- 📖 Matthew 18:4–5
- 📖 Mark 5:41
- 📖 Mark 9:36–37
- 📖 Luke 9:6
- 📖 Luke 9:11
- 📖 Luke 9:42
- 📖 Luke 18:15–17
- 📖 Acts 4:22

Additional Analysis

For further investigation, read Matthew 15:21-28

1. How did this woman represent her crisis to Jesus? Do you think she outlined the urgency of it well?

2. Why do you think she called Jesus "Lord, the Son of David"?

3. Have you ever felt that someone was trying to push you away and give you the cold shoulder? How did it make you feel?

4. List the barriers that this woman had to overcome before getting the action that she needed.

5. How did she get over each of the hurdles?

6. In your opinion, why did this woman not give up after Jesus ignored her?

7. How did Jesus pay tribute to her?

8. What does this story tell us about faith?

9. Have you ever really wanted something and thought it was right, but it fell through or God closed the door and you later discovered that, had you kept going, it would have ended in disaster or failure?

10. Is there something right now in your life that you have been believing and praying for that sometimes feels like it will never happen? Describe it.

11. How can we show the same kind of persistent faith that this woman had so that we also receive our answers?

12. This is not just a story of wonderful healing; it is also a story of the love and tenacity of a mother who never gave up. As parents, we need to not give up on our kids, but always lift them up to God. What do the following verses tell us about children and prayer?
    a. Genesis 24:60
    b. Ezra 8:21
    c. Mark 10:13
    d. Acts 21:5

13. Write out a special prayer for your children and say it daily. If you do not have any children of your own, then pray for children that you know through your family, friends, church or co-workers.

Memory Verse

"So encourage each other and give each other strength, just as you are doing now" (1 Thessalonians 5:11 NCV).

Newfound Facts

_____

_____

_____

_____

_____

_____

_____

_____

_____

_____

_____

_____

_____

_____

M Lorene Kimura

Whatever you do, work at it with all your heart, as working for the Lord, not for men.

Colossians 3:23

8

Leadership and Hospitality

He used the businesswoman

(Acts 16:6-15, and 40)

Lydia, by today's standards, would definitely be considered a "women's libber" or a feminist. She was a very successful businesswoman who manufactured and sold a type of cloth prized for its royal purple color. There is no clarification of whether she was a widow, a single mother or simply unmarried. We do know that she was the head of her household, which included being responsible for adults, children and slaves. She had a very strong faith and was very influential with her family, friends and servants, demonstrating to them through her example the need for baptism. She was a woman who always remembered the importance of the Sabbath and consistently honoured it. She was a very generous person and demonstrated a real spirit of hospitality to Paul and his friends even after their imprisonment.

Lydia was not one who came to the Lord through desperation; rather, society would say she had it all together. Since early biblical times, women were only allowed to take an active role in the running of their own households, so her situation would have been considered unique. The day-to-day operation of business was designated for the men—after all; they were believed to be the intelligent ones. Lydia made herself an exception to this rule and found herself in an extraordinary situation because, even though she was a woman, she was the one who sold clothes made from her deep-dyed purple fabric.

The cost of production plus the time involved to create this highly sought-after material was the cause of its extremely high price. The dye for the cloth came from a shellfish. The juice was white while it was in the veins of the fish, but exposure to the sun changed the liquid into bright purple and red colors. It took a great deal of work to harvest enough shellfish to dye even one garment, so it was not a simple procedure. The very rich, royalty and the Roman senators were the only ones who could actually afford her clothes, which, in turn, made her very influential and financially very well off. Even with all of her wealth, she remained a down-to-earth person, making sure that she used her great wealth to take care of her family and household servants.

Apparently, there were not enough Jews in Philippi to warrant the building of a synagogue. Therefore, it was the custom for the people to find a spot outside the city at the riverside to gather and worship God. Lydia was instrumental in gathering the women to meet and pray outside the town. Hers was the only name mentioned, so it has been determined that she must have been the group's leader. Lydia was a strong worshipper who believed in the God of Israel and would offer her praises to him.

Lydia was not a follower of Jesus until one day when Paul showed up at the meeting and started speaking with the women. She became very attentive and absorbed with what Paul was teaching. Acts 16:14 tells us, "now a certain woman named Lydia heard us. She was a seller of purple from the city of Thyatira, who worshiped God. The Lord opened her heart to heed the things spoken by Paul" (NKVJ). After listening carefully to Paul's words, she now had a decision to make; should she take heed of the words of this man or dismiss them as words only for the workers and the slaves? (God has given us the ability to make choices, yet he will never force us into a decision.) Lydia chose to hear the words of Paul with openness and a desire to learn all that she could. She was the first Christian convert reported in Europe.

As with many new believers, Lydia was anxious to share Jesus with others. Today, new believers may feel the same, but think that the only way to make it possible is to leave their jobs, their families and their friends to go off to some faraway land as a missionary. Lydia did not leave her position, her family or her friends but, after her salvation, she wasted no time before starting to serve God. She remained in her current situation and used her status as the basis of her ministry. As a new and excited believer, she shared her new love with her household. As a result, Lydia, her entire family and her servants were all baptized.

The next thing Lydia did was to offer her servants, her home and large amounts of her money to the Apostles in gratitude for Christ's gift of salvation. Her home must have been very large to accommodate Paul, Silas and the very large entourage that was travelling with them. Her immense generosity was evident as she informed them that they were welcome to stay in her home for as long as they would like. When you think of it, this really was a very generous offer. Can you imagine having several people staying in your home for a week, a month or maybe even a year? Lydia not only offered her home; she also used it as the new church of Philippi. Many people came to meet there and many received salvation.

Paul perceived that she was a spiritual leader to whom others looked for guidance. It did not matter that she was a woman. What mattered was her love for God and her willingness to serve. Later, while in prison, Paul wrote to the Philippians and mentioned women who had worked hard to help spread the word about Jesus to the people. Philippians 4:3: "And I urge you also, true companion, help these women who labored with me in the gospel, with Clement also, and the rest of my fellow workers, whose names are in the Book of Life" (NKJV).

Lydia remained available for God to use her. She did not become haughty about how much money she had, although she certainly could have; rather, she worked to have others come to know Jesus—the same Jesus whom she had come to know and grown to love and pursue. Being a success for God holds no shame. In fact, he desires for us to be successful. However, our reaction to that success is more important; do we share it willingly or do we become high and mighty about it? Lydia had a gift of wonderful creativity, an ability to run a business and a strong work ethic. She also demonstrated a great willingness to share the success that she had earned to help others.

Colossians 3:23 says, "In all the work you are doing, work the best you can. Work as if you were doing it for the Lord, not for people."

(NCV). We need to utilize our God-given talents in the best way we can, ensuring that they bring honour to God. We must remember that we are accountable for what we accomplish and what we do with those accomplishments. Luke 12:48 states, "From everyone who has been given much, much will be demanded and from the one who has been trusted with much, much more will be expected"(NIV). Lydia continued to use her talents and her gifts for the glory of God. She remained extremely generous to her family, her servants, the teachers of Jesus and anyone else who wanted to learn of the Risen King.

Turn Your Heart

As Paul shared the message of a living God, his words were able to reach down deep into Lydia's heart and change her life forever. Consequently, because this one woman opened her heart and allowed the Holy Spirit to work in and through her, many other lives were impacted. Are you prepared to release yourself to the Holy Spirit with that level of obedience so that he may work in you to affect others around you?

We all know people who need to come to know Jesus, but what are we willing to do about it? Proverbs 23:26 says, "My son, give me your heart, and let your eyes observe my ways" (NKJV). How can they give their hearts if they do not hear the Word?

Think of people you know who need to have a personal relationship with Jesus. Make a list of their names and honestly and regularly pray for them. Keep your prayer list in a visible place so that you will remember to pray for them during the day.

Pray that God will use you as his representative as he opens the door for you to share the Word and be a witness for him.

Lydia was obedient to the teaching of the Word and became an energetic and influential leader for Jesus. You can do it too! God desires for us to take that step out of the box, follow it with a leap of faith and be geared up to serve him. Are you ready?

Let's Pray

Lord, I bring these people on my prayer list to you. I pray, Lord, that you will open doors so that I and others may share your love with them that they may come to know you. Lord, you said that he who plants and he who waters are one, and each one will receive his own reward according to his own labour. I pray, Lord, that I will have the tenacity to labour and use the talents and gifts that you have given me to the best of my ability. I pray, Lord, that as I use these talents I will keep a humble spirit, always remembering that they are not my own but come from you.

Lord, you place opportunities before me, and I pray that I will recognize them and not be afraid to take the step of faith to share you. We never know if we are the seed planter, a little bit of fertilizer or the one you will use to lead this person into a personal relationship with you. Your Word says in 1 Corinthians 3:7, "neither he who plants is anything, nor he who waters, but it is you (God) who gives the increase" (NKJV). We do know that we can trust you to use every situation for your glory if only we let you.

Future Study Scriptures

- Exodus 22:28 (MSG)
- Numbers 7:10
- Numbers 34:18)
- Judges 8:6 (MSG)
- 1 Kings 20:19
- 2 Chronicles 12:6 (MSG)
- Ezra 5:5 (MSG

- Proverbs 14:28 (MSG)
- Isaiah 55:4
- Matthew 9:37
- Matthew 20:28
- Luke 10:2
- Romans 12:13

Additional Analysis

For further investigation, read Acts 16:6-15, and 40

1. What was Lydia's hometown? (One of the seven churches of Asia was located there.)

2. What was noteworthy about Lydia's profession?

3. Paul and his friends arrived in Philippi on the Sabbath, and they found a group of women worshipping outside the town. As you read these verses, describe the picture that comes to your mind.

4. From Paul's reaction to this group, what can we determine were his views on women?

5. The Bible says in Acts 16:14 that Lydia's heart was opened. How do you interpret the words "the Lord opened her heart"?

6. Reading Acts 16:14, we see our first description of Lydia as a person. What kind of person do you imagine her to be? In one or two sentences, how would you describe yourself?

7. What is the significance of the fact that Lydia was not only the first convert in Europe, but was also female?

8. As soon as she became a believer, she immediately did two things (v. 15). What were they?

9. Lydia showed great hospitality to Paul and his friends. What difference did this make to them?

10. Why was she so anxious for them to stay with her?

11. Her new ministry was influential to two groups of people. Who were they?

12. John 15:1-16 talks about the fruit and the vine. How did Lydia's life and works create fruit in those around her?

13. Usually the words from Luke 12:48 are considered to be directed toward those in a pastoral ministry. Do you think that is the only interpretation for them? If not, please explain.

14. How does the story of Lydia affect women becoming involved in ministry today? How does it affect you?

15. What about this story encouraged or especially spoke to you?

Memory Verse

"In all the work you are doing, work the best you can. Work as if you were doing for the Lord and not for people" (Colossians 3:23).

Newfound Facts

_____

_____

_____

_____

_____

_____

_____

_____

And whatever you do in word or deed, do all in the name of the Lord Jesus, giving thanks to God the Father through Him.

Colossians 3:17 (NKJV)

9

Loyalty

He used the wealthy

(Acts 16, Luke 24)

It was not the custom for women in biblical times to be front and centre. Therefore, the women who followed Jesus held no aspirations or expectations of being part of his inner circle or being given the title of apostle. All they wanted was to serve him in any way they could and generally just be near him to hear his teachings.

I am sure there must have been some eyebrows raised when men saw these women so close to Jesus. Everyone knew that a woman's place was in the home, supporting her husband, caring for the children and staying out of sight unless called upon. In fact, men felt that women were such second-class citizens that by no means were they ever allowed an education, nor would any of the prominent leaders or teachers ever allow a woman to sit at their feet for an opportunity to listen or learn. There were instructions given to men to not even speak to a woman unless her husband was present, so she would not lead them into adultery.

For these women disciples, things were somewhat different. They had seen and felt enough to know that there was something compelling about this man named Jesus. What he was teaching and sharing made so much sense that they had to follow him and hear more. Whatever questions or concerns they had were not enough to keep them away; rather, the opposite occurred—they were drawn closer to him. As time passed, they became active participants in Christ's ministry and gave whatever and wherever they could. Acts 1:14 tells us "They all met together and were constantly united in prayer, along with Mary the mother of Jesus, several other women, and the brothers of Jesus" (NLT).

Joanna was one of these women. Although there is not a lot written about her, we do know that she was a wealthy woman. She was married to a man named Chuza, who looked after Herod's vast estates. Because of her husband's position, she was accustomed to and comfortable with many of the worldly possessions and customs in Herod's palace. She was also very confident when it came to dealing with large sums of money.

Joanna was one of several women who accompanied Jesus and she showed great generosity from her own assets. Luke 8:3 says, "Joanna, the wife of Chuza, Herod's business manager; Susanna; and many others who were contributing their own resources to support Jesus and his disciples" (NLT). Although we do not know the particulars, we know that Jesus had healed her from some kind of medical condition. Some theologians think it may have been a form of mental illness. Luke 8:2 states that the group surrounding Jesus included, "certain women who had been healed of evil spirits or infirmities" (NKJV). Now, for the first time in a very long time, these women had a taste of life without pain or anxiety. They now had a picture of how life should be and they wanted to be a part of it. Listening to Jesus, they discovered details they had never thought possible. After Joanna personally experienced healing, her dedication to this man named Jesus was unstoppable. She was one of the women who spoke to the disciples following Jesus' resurrection. From all these things, we can believe that she was one of the women to whom the Bible refers as the "many women" who followed or travelled with Jesus during his time on earth.

No doubt, there were times when she was nervous about what would happen to Jesus and his followers if Herod decided to go after them. After all, she knew how extremely troubled she was when Herod executed John the Baptist, a holy man, when he spoke the truth. She understood that her love of Jesus put her own life in danger, yet she continued to share her story. Did she think that maybe if she spoke about Jesus enough she could influence and change Herod's way of thinking?

Her husband's position would have allowed Joanna the freedom to walk around the courtyard and the palace as she pleased, consequently giving her full contact with all of the servants. Because of her newfound passion, she most likely shared the news about her love of Jesus with any of the staff and slaves who would listen. With her excitement bubbling over, I can only guess that if they did not listen the first time, she would continue to share Jesus each time she met them until, at the very least, some believed. Joanna must have realized that any time Herod chose he could turn on her, even calling her a traitor, for which the punishment would be an immediate death sentence. She never seemed to mind the risks that her faith required, and there is no evidence to show that she ever diverted from it.

We never hear what her husband's thoughts and feelings were about this, but we can assume that they were not good because he was loyal to Herod. However, even her husband's feelings on this matter did not sway Joanna. She was going to follow Jesus at all costs. Joanna had faith and trust in Jesus and the work he was doing. She was determined to remain a vocal part of his work no matter what the consequences might be. Scholars think that Chuza may have even lost his position due to his inability to control his wife, but there is no proof of this allegation.

It must have caused Joanna great anguish when Herod joked and made fun of Jesus as he turned him over to Pilate. Can you hear Herod now? "Oh, Joanna, look at your Jesus now. If he is so good, why doesn't he perform a miracle and save himself?" Herod most likely took great pleasure in taunting Joanna and probably went on and on with a jab-jab-jab and a dig-dig-dig as if to say, "You stupid woman, you are so deluded." He would undoubtedly have kept up his fun until she wanted to scream at him or even lash out and strike him to make him stop. There is no documentation of this, but we can only imagine how Herod would have taken great joy in someone else's emotional pain. He was, after all, the same man who decapitated another man and brought his head in on a platter to entertain his guests.

When they killed Jesus, Joanna's pain must have been indescribable. She believed in this man; he had healed her and she had seen him heal others and perform many miracles. She knew that he was more than just another man, and she trusted and believed in him. It is difficult to even imagine the agony that she and the other women felt for him and for the pain he was enduring as they followed him to his crucifixion. She could see—and in her mind she could feel—the pain and suffering that he was undergoing as they tortured him even before they hung him on the cross. She was a witness as they drove the spikes through his hands and feet and then forced him to hang in agony as those huge spikes tore at his flesh. To top off her emotions, which by now would have been running wild, the earth began to shake from an earthquake and darkness covered the land. It makes you wonder how any one human being could have withstood all of this in just one day.

We know that the disciples could not handle it, because they left and even denied him. Yet the group of women did not run. They stayed with Jesus and even tried to get closer to him, perhaps to try to be a comfort to him. Luke 23:49 says "But all His acquaintances, and the women who were with him in Galilee stood at a distance watching these things." (NKJV)

Even after Jesus took his last breath, they still did not leave; rather, they followed along to the tomb and saw the grave where they thought the body of Jesus would remain forever. They must have felt totally lost, now thinking, "This is it, the end. They have killed him! Now what will happen?" Fighting exhaustion, they felt that they still needed to prepare the spices required to make the body ready for its final resting place. Completion of the entire preparation had to be done before sundown so that they could obey the law and rest on the Sabbath. These amazing women were so faithful to Jesus that they wanted to show him this final respect, while, at the same time, remaining faithful to God and the Holy Law concerning rest on the Sabbath.

Can you imagine the gamut of emotions felt when Joanna and the other women went to the grave, only to find it empty? "He has been stolen! How could anyone do this? I do not believe it!" Imagine the confusion as they all ran around looking inside, outside and all around the tomb.

They would have felt disgust and disbelief that anyone would be so low as to do this. Had they not humiliated him enough? When they finally stopped for a moment to take a breath, only then would they have seen the angel standing there, asking, "Why do you seek the living among the dead?" (Luke 24:5 NKJV).

God honoured Joanna's faith and trust by allowing her to be one of the first to see that Jesus had risen. Frustration would have mixed with the excitement of this news as she ran to tell the disciples what she and the others had not only learned, but also seen—only to be mocked in return. You can hear her almost yelling at them, "Come on, fellows, you have to listen. No one could make this up! I am not just some stupid woman. I know what I have seen. I know what I have heard. You have to trust us. Jesus is really alive!" How hard it must have been not to be believed.

Joanna had been with Jesus through the good and the bad times. She had seen him perform miracles, she had heard him teach the people and she had brought provisions for the journeys. She may have thought that it was all over when she saw him tortured and hung on the cross and finally placed in the grave. Yet, she was at the grave, equipped with spices and ointments ready to anoint the body, choosing once more to help provide for the man whom she so loved. Her greatest virtue was her faith and her ability to keep looking forward to the big picture even though she was ridiculed and harassed by Herod, her husband and even the disciples.

Turn Your Heart

Joanna trusted and believed in Jesus. She did not just "feel" her beliefs, but illustrated her loyalty with her actions by providing what she could for his ministry. She also demonstrated it with her speech as she openly shared her belief in the work that Jesus was doing with others.

Do you put your actions where your heart is, or do you think, "I am only one person, so what could I possibly do?"

It is easy to talk about Jesus with those who know and love him, but what about with those who do not? Can you even mention his name to them?

Do you openly share Jesus with others who do not already know him? What about that neighbour who you know is struggling, or the co-worker who tells you her troubles and seems to be really looking for answers?

Do you really want to get involved, or do you want to sit back in your home and watch television, feeling sorry for someone else's situation but not believing that you can do anything about it?

Do you want the boldness to take a step of faith?

Do you want to be able to give to the various areas your local church supports in your city or to a non-profit for overseas work?

If we answer yes to these questions, then are we demonstrating it with our actions? If no, then why not, and how can we? What is stopping us from taking part in Christ's work to reach the multitudes? It may not always take dollars but it may require our time or our talents. We need to have Jesus reveal to us what it is that he would have us do to touch others.

If you are honest and want to help, then take a step of faith and ask God where or how it is that he would have you provide help.

Let's Pray

Lord, help me fulfill what you have designed to be my part to further your kingdom. If finances are what you desire, then help me to see where they are to come from and how to give with a willing heart. Help me to have the boldness of Joanna. Even in the face of danger, she was willing to proclaim her love for you. Through ridicule and condemnation, help me to remember your love and your goodness and to show them to those whom I meet. Joanna knew you, trusted you and honoured you, and you, in turn, blessed her by allowing her to see the empty tomb and discover that you were alive.

I pray for that same visible and growing trust in my life. Help me to stay focused on the great reward of eternal life with you even as I endure trials and tribulations that I now think are too great to bear. Help me to see that, in the light of eternity, these problems will someday seem small and maybe even insignificant. You promised to never leave or forsake me and your grace is sufficient for all my needs even when I feel that I am at the end of my rope and the knot is slipping. Thank you, Jesus.

Future Study Scriptures

- 📖 Matthew 28:19
- 📖 Luke 12:30; 24:47
- 📖 2 Corinthians 12:7 (MSG)
- 📖 Galatians 6:6
- 📖 Hebrews 13:5
- 📖 James 1:12
- 📖 1Peter 1:6–7

Additional Analysis

For further investigation, read Acts 16, Luke 24 and Colossians 3:17

1. Many of us have experienced, in some form or fashion, a healing that society would not consider natural. It may have been from depression, a serious illness or a life-changing situation. Who was there for you to help you out of those times?

2. Joanna and the others demonstrated their appreciation for their healing. What can we do? What should we do?

3. What do you think Joanna's life was like after she started to associate with Jesus—both when she was with Jesus and when she was at home?

4. Why would she continue supporting Jesus and his men when she must have had to go through so much at home?

5. Why do you think the disciples did not want to believe what these women were trying to tell them about the empty grave?

6. How would you describe Joanna to a group of people who had never heard of her?

7. Looking at the following scriptures, describe how we are to move on and out for God.
    a. Psalm 138:3
    b. Acts 13:46
    c. Hebrews 13:16
    d. Proverbs 28:1
    e. Ephesians 6:20

8. How do you think we achieve this boldness?

9. With the attitudes toward women being so negative in those times, why do you think Jesus helped and worked with so many women?

10. Do you think these women have an influence on women in ministry today?

11. We all have opportunities to minister to others in a variety of ways throughout each day. Who do you minister to throughout the course of your day?

12. Can you think of a time in your life when you had to stop and move over so that Jesus could come in and do the work? Elaborate.

13. In what ways, other than through our finances, can we serve the cause of Christ?

Memory Verse

"So give yourself completely to God, Stand against the devil, and the devil will run from you" (James 4:7 NCV).

Newfound Facts

_____

_____

_____

_____

_____

_____

_____

_____

_____

_____

_____

_____

_____

_____

_____

_____

❧ But you, O Lord, are a God full of compassion,
and gracious longsuffering
and abundant mercy and truth. ❧

Psalm 86.15 (NKJV)

10

A Surprise Gift

He used the poor

(Luke 7:11-16)

Nain, usually a very quiet town, was located near the sea of Galilee. The name *Nain* means "pleasant or delightful," but on this day, it was anything but that. On this particular day, you could hear the cries and wails of a mother who was mourning the death of her only son. Her husband had passed away previously, and losing her son left her with no chance of any inheritance. She herself would have nothing; she was now destitute.

This lady was in for some very desperate times. As a widow with no family to care for her, she faced a very dark future. This situation would lead some to resort to stealing, prostitution or even slavery just to survive. This was not what she had dreamed of as a little girl, but what else could she do? Where would she go? These were the questions facing this mother. She had no idea that today Jesus would change her life in a way far greater than she could ever imagine.

Two very distinct groups of people were in town that day, and each was unknowingly walking toward the other. One was the mother who was going to bury her son, and her cries and the cries of those with her resonating throughout the town. All of the hopes this mother had placed in her son—all of her dreams for him and all of her dreams for herself—were gone. I can empathize with this mother losing her dreams for her son, because I remember how I felt when our family received another call from my brother informing us of a very tragic accident that had taken the life of his youngest son. You realize at that moment that all of the dreams this person had for his life (as well as the ones you had for him) have abruptly ended, still unfinished. Like the widow, the joy that this person is meeting his Heavenly Father and reuniting with other family members who have gone on before is the farthest thing from your mind. All you can see at that moment is what you have lost.

Coming toward this woman was another very large crowd that was following Jesus. They had just witnessed the healing of the centurion's servant and their excitement and joyous cheers also carried for miles around. This parade of people felt not the sting of death but the joy of life. As they passed the first crowd, Jesus saw this devastated mother and he felt empathy for her and instructed her not to cry. "When the Lord saw her, He had compassion on her and said to her, 'Do not weep'" (Luke 7:13 NKJV).

Do not cry? "But Lord, do you not understand that I have already buried my husband and now have to bury my only son, leaving me alone and destitute? How can you say 'Do not cry'?"

Because she did not know Jesus, she did not know what he could do and what he would do for her.

Charles Swindoll writes in his book, *The Continuation of Something Great,* that the differences between these two groups illustrate that our Saviour does not demand that we fit into a set pattern in order to receive his help. He does not restrain his compassion because we fail to meet our "good deed quota" or because we do not say the right words or forget to follow the correct ritual.

When Jesus saw the widow, he felt compassion for her. This was not just a casual "Oh, that's too bad," but rather, the type of compassion that goes deep into your innermost being. The Greek translation says that he was "moved in his inward parts." This type of compassion gets under your skin and eats at you, making you feel almost sick to your stomach. You might have sensed it when you watched television shows about disasters or orphaned children with flies on their faces and distended bellies due to poor nutrition.

As Jesus looked at this mother, he felt a deep crushing sorrow for her that went right down into the pit of his stomach. He saw a person who really needed him—someone who did not know who he was and, therefore, was expecting nothing from him. Jesus not only saw her grief over the loss of her son, but he understood the social status and the circumstances in which she would now have to live.

Once, a mother sent her little girl to the corner store to pick up a few groceries. She took longer than expected to return and the mother chastised her because she was worried. When she was questioned about where she had been and why it had taken her so long, she explained to her mother that she had run into one of her little friends. She further explained that her friend was crying because she had broken her favourite doll. Her mother then asked her if she had stopped to try to help her to fix it, only to hear her daughter say no, that she had stopped to cry with her.

Compassion filled this little girl as she wept with her friend over her broken doll. Jesus felt this kind of compassion for the widow.

According to Israelite law, anyone touching a dead body would become unclean. Did that stop Jesus? Did he say, "I will have to get gloves before I can go near him?" Did he hesitate? No! He felt great compassion for this woman and he was going to help her—now! He went right up to the young man's coffin, reached out and, with the power and authority that belongs to him, said, "'Young man, I say to you, get up!' With that the young man sat up and began to talk and Jesus gave him back to his mother" (Luke 7:14-15 NIV).

Can you imagine the look on this mother's face? The entire crowd began cheering and yelling, calling Jesus a "great prophet." They had heard of this happening before, but that was in the time of Elijah the prophet and that was hundreds of years ago.

At that moment, an array of emotions must have run through this mother—joy, excitement and an initial disbelief of what had just happened. She may have thought that she was seeing things, for she too had heard of people being raised from the dead, but that was long ago, in the days of her ancestors.

Still afraid to believe it, she must have thought, "Can it really happen to me? I am nothing like the Shunammite woman—she was wealthy and very important. I am nothing; I am dirt-poor and insignificant." Yet, God does not see anyone as insignificant. Each of us is more valuable to him that we can ever imagine.

Why would Jesus choose to help this woman? She was not like some of the other women who demonstrated great faith and trust in God. This woman did not even know who Jesus was. How could she repay him? She had no way of understanding that when those with her raised their praises to God and came to know him in that new and special way, he was paid in full and there was no debt recorded. We cannot buy the love that God wants to pour out on us, nor could we ever monetarily repay Jesus for the sacrifice he made. All God wants is for us to come and have a personal relationship with him so that he can shower us with his grace, mercy and blessing.

In this town, where everyone had felt nothing but sadness for this poor widowed mother, a new joy and rejoicing could now be heard. All of those with her were applauding and shouting, "God has come to help his people." This woman must have become one of Jesus' best witnesses in Nain. After all, everyone whom she met who offered sympathy for her son would only hear her exclaim, "He is alive! Jesus arrived in Nain and God raised him to life. Praise God, I have him back!"

Turn Your Heart

This woman may have become poor through the death of her son, but with one touch from Jesus she received a life restored that was richer than gold. God loves us too much to leave us in the pit of hopelessness that we may feel that we are now in. Keep praising him. If we know

Jesus already, we have an advantage over this woman. If you don't, then this is the time to ask him to come into your heart and forgive you of all past sins. He is real and he is alive, so it is important to keep leaning on him. He knows what we need, and he will supply all of our needs if we just trust in him.

Sometimes the Lord works miracles on our behalf, showing us mercy and giving back what we may have lost. Not all miracles are huge in comparison to the one this widow received, but all the same, they are miracles meant just for us.

One miracle I remember that was just for me happened while I was travelling out of town. At some point during a one-hour period, I lost my wallet on a very busy downtown street in a major city just hours before I was to catch a flight home. Without the wallet, I could not get onto the flight because I had no identification. With the help of a wonderful friend, I retraced my footsteps and, after asking everyone in the businesses where I had been, one terrific security person said, "Yes, I have it." Someone had turned it in and it was complete, with not one penny missing. That was a miracle from God. I caught my flight with 30 minutes to spare. We can do nothing to earn this kind of favour, but when it does happen, we can rejoice loudly from the mountaintops, telling everyone that Jesus is alive and that he is here among his people.

Has Jesus shown you a miracle? When you need a miracle, pray with the expectation of receiving.

"But when you ask, you must believe and not doubt, because the one who doubts is like a wave of the sea, blown and tossed by the wind" (James 1:6 NIV).

We do not want to live in the past, but it is good to look back at what God has done for us and how he has helped us to grow. Remember, he brought us to this place on purpose, and it does not matter who we are or were, but who we are becoming. We may be poor in finances or in spirit, but Jesus can move us from that spot if only we will let him.

Let's Pray

Lord, help me to focus on you and what you are doing in my life. There are times that I feel so low in spirit and the pathway ahead seems so dark. I know that you are there even when the storm clouds are overhead, bills need to be paid, my pocketbook is empty and there is no hope in sight. I know that I need to trust you, turn all my concerns over to you and let you help me to get through. I know that you can help me if I will only let you in. There is no such thing as an accident, and you have brought me to this place on purpose. I need to remember that it does not matter who I am, but rather, who it is that I am becoming. I know that you want me to be a person who will glorify you; teach me to be the person who you desire me to be. Just as you raised this widow's son, you can raise to life the dreams that I have allowed to die or be pushed aside. Show me, Lord, what it is that you want to bring to life and what it is that you want me to do for you. Help me, Lord, to keep my heart open for you to come in and move me from where I am.

Future Study Scriptures

- Deuteronomy 28:1
- Psalm 21:3
- Zechariah 10:1
- John 12:17
- Acts 13:30
- Romans 6:29
- Romans 8:28

Additional Analysis

For further investigation, read Luke 7:11-6

1. This woman was not asking Jesus for help; in fact, she did not know him, so why would he stop to help her out of the blue? Besides, he was with an entirely different group of people at the time.

2. The story tells us that Jesus had "great compassion" for this woman. What does this term mean to you?

3. Why do you think Jesus was so willing to help this lady even without being asked, while previously he tried to turn away the Canaanite woman who was so desperate?

4. Jesus healed this woman's son even though she was not a woman of great faith. What does this tell you about God's love for people?

5. If you were a newspaper reporter describing the events of the day, how would you report this story?

6. Each scripture below describes God's compassion. Read each one and describe what it means to you:
   a. Psalm 145:8
   b. 2 Kings 13:23
   c. 2 Chronicles 30:9

7. Has there been a time in your life when God showed you compassion that you did not expect?

8. Have you ever experienced the type of compassion that made you feel that you just had to get up and take action? Explain.

9. What do you imagine the rest of this woman's life was like? Do you think she returned to her old ways and beliefs, or did she follow and praise Jesus?

10. What about her son—how do you think he reacted when he was told the story? Do you think he even believed it? (It does sound far-fetched, after all.) Think about what you would think if someone told you such a story.

Memory Verse

"But when you ask God, you must believe and not doubt. Anyone who doubts is like a wave in the sea, blown up and down by the wind" (James 1:6 NCV).

Newfound Facts

_____

_____

_____

_____

_____

_____

_____

_____

_____

_____

_____

_____

_____

_____

_____

_____

❧ *And he commanded them, saying, "Thus you shall act in the fear of the LORD, faithfully and with a loyal heart"* ❧

2 Chronicles 19:9 (NKJV)

Prostitute Redeemed

He used the desirable

Joshua 2:1-24; 6:17-25

Rahab—a desirable woman? When the people of Jericho talked about her (and talk they did!), desirable was not a description that they used. Harlot or *zonah* (prostitute) were more likely the terms to be heard from these townsfolk as they discussed Rahab. How then, can we call her desirable? Obviously, she was desirable to men, but more importantly, she was desirable to God because of her willing heart that was ready to serve him.

She was a prostitute, but a prostitute with a destiny. She turned her life around, and God was able to use her in a great and wonderful way that helped to save the lives of the Israelite spies as well as of her own family.

The location of Rahab's home (or place of business) with its high roof provided a good vantage point for viewing the city and was close to the city gates, giving quick access to the outside. Archaeologists say that the double walls of Jericho were 12 to 15 feet apart, allowing just enough room to squeeze a house between them. The flax on her roof points to the fact that she and her family most likely were growing flax for the linen workers to make clothing for the priests and the upper class. It also suggests that she was probably from a poor family, because only the poorer classes of people worked on the farming end of the linen business.

Maybe this is why Rahab started her own personal business of taking care of men's sexual needs. Perhaps she wanted more than farming in her future. Maybe her goal was to earn money to help her family. Then again, maybe she felt trapped doing what she was doing and could not see any escape. We may never know the real reason why she was prostituting. However, we do know for sure that she was a working girl who knew that God was different from any of the gods of her people, and we know that she wanted to let him lead her down a new road.

When the two spies found Rahab's place, they recognized it as a perfect hideout. The very nature of her business ensured that the house always had a large number of people coming and going, so it would be easier to remain incognito and make a quick and clean getaway. They must have known, too, that she would have to be discreet about who came and went. Too bad their plans did not go the way they expected. Someone did see them enter, and before they knew it, the king's men were pounding on Rahab's door, ordering her to turn over the spies immediately.

Now what? Can you remember a time when your mother asked you to do something and you just knew that you had better do it fast because she was really serious? That is how it was with the king's men. They meant right now! She had a big decision to make—if she hid the men, then she was turning her back on her people, her king, her city and above all, her gods. She was risking everything, because if she was caught in the lie, the punishment for treason would be death. Why, with all this at stake, would she risk it? Who were these men to her?

We read the answer in Joshua 2:10-11: "We have heard how the LORD dried up the water of the Red Sea for you when you came out of Egypt, and what you did to the two kings of the Amorites who were on the other side of the Jordan, Sihon and Og, whom you utterly destroyed. And as soon as we heard these things, our hearts melted; neither did there remain any more courage in anyone because of you, for the LORD your God, He is God in heaven above and on earth beneath" (NKJV).

Rahab basically told these men, "Your God is everything and my god is nothing. Furthermore, nothing can stand in the way of your God and his purposes." She acknowledged the fact that God had given her land to them and that her land as she knew it was lost. Remember, this was a split-second decision; the king's men were standing at the door demanding that she turn the spies over to them at once!

"The men? Oh yes, they were here all right, but they are gone now. If you go quickly you should be able to catch them, and, oh, yes, they went that way" (Joshua 2:5). Meanwhile, the spies were hiding on the roof under some of the flax that she was drying. Good thing neither of them had hay fever and started sneezing!

Rahab had only one request of these spies—if she helped them, would they remember her when they took over the city? She demonstrated how important her family was to her by asking the men to also grant safety to them. She knew that there was no one in her city who could save her, and why would anyone want to? After all, she was just a harlot. She would need help from the outside, from the very ones coming to conquer.

It is the same today; we cannot save ourselves, only the intervention of the Lord can save us. The two spies promised her protection if only she would tie a scarlet cord in her window. Historians cannot seem to agree if the cord that let the spies down from the roof became the window cord, or if it was one of a smaller thread. Wherever the cord came from, this woman was not about to procrastinate even for a moment. As soon as she let the two spies down, she immediately placed the cord in its new setting

Scripture views Rahab's dealings with the spies as faith in action. When Rahab was talking with the spies, she was acknowledging their God and the miracles that he had performed for the children of Israel. God's reputation preceded the two spies' arrival, and she had heard all about it. She knew about God's power and she seemed to also have known about his wonderful grace. She acknowledged him as the Lord and even called him the Lord their God. Even though she may not have understood everything about God, she knew that there was something different about this God compared to the gods of her people.

How is it that this woman, who lived in a land that worshipped false gods, who was herself a prostitute and whose family was very poor, would know so much about the Lord? Had the spies told her? Personally, I do not think that they would share their hearts, hopes and desires with a stranger, let alone someone from the land of their enemies. Would you tell your enemy your deepest dreams and desires?

Just as the Woman at the Well knew that there was something different about Jesus, Rahab knew that there was something different about these men and knew that they must represent a God who required honour. Is it possible that, just as the Holy Spirit entered Lydia's heart to hear Paul's words from God, Rahab's heart opened in a similar fashion, allowing her to discover the true God? Could God do a saving work of faith in the heart of such a sinful woman just as he had done for so many sinners before her and has continued to do since? The writer to the Hebrews reminds us, "By faith the prostitute Rahab . . ." (Hebrews 11:31 NIV).

She may not have completely understood why, but she chose to trust the true God instead of the false gods that her people worshipped. She trusted that God would bless her for taking action to protect the spies. She trusted him to protect her and her family when the invasion of the city took place. She ultimately trusted him to take care of her forever and to send a Saviour for her.

Can you imagine what was going on in the minds of those in that house as the trumpets started sounding and people started praising? What about when those two thick walls that surrounded the once-great city began collapsing? The noise must have been deafening from the walls crashing and the cheers of the people who came rushing in. As they were being overtaken, they could hear the fighting and the cries of her people, the barking of dogs, the donkeys' braying and the other animals calling out in fright. The heat from the blazing fires was scorching as they burned her town to ruins.

When Jericho was destroyed, no doubt good people perished alongside the evil. The rich perished alongside the poor. The well-educated perished alongside the uneducated. The one thing that these so-called religious people had in common was that they had turned against the true God's coming kingdom. Where were Rahab and her family through all of this? They were tucked inside her home, protected and just waiting for the word that it was safe to come out. I can imagine some of the children in the house were crying with fear from all of the noise and action that they could hear; but still they waited and Rahab trusted until they were liberated and invited to live among the Israelites.

There would be a great reward for her act of unselfishness, faith and trust. Rahab found spiritual salvation and physical protection, but that was not the end; she received a good husband and a son who became very active in his work for God's kingdom. She would eventually become the great, great, great, great grandmother of King David, and do you know what that means? Yes, Jesus is a direct descendant of Rahab. It just goes to show that when you allow God to get your heart, he can do anything to and for you, no matter your colour, race, age or status.

Turn Your Heart

Greater than the fact that Rahab found physical protection for her obedience to God, she also received protection from spiritual and eternal harm. Here is a woman who was actively taking part in adultery through her prostitution. The other women of the city looked down on her, and the men who so often visited her bed ignored her. "Rahab the harlot" are three words that now describe a woman who loved God, believed in him and followed him, even putting herself at great risk. We are very blessed because "Even before he made the world, God loved us and chose us in Christ to be holy and without fault in his eyes. God decided in advance to adopt us into his own family by bringing us to himself through Jesus Christ. This is what he wanted to do, and it gave him great pleasure. So we praise God for the glorious grace he has poured out on us who belong to his dear Son. He is so rich in kindness and grace that he purchased our freedom with the blood of his Son and forgave our sins. He has showered his kindness on us, along with all wisdom and understanding" (Ephesians 1:4-8 NLT).

God touched Rahab's heart and by his grace transformed her into a new creature. "Therefore, if anyone is in Christ, he is a new creation; old things have passed away; behold, all things have become new" (2 Corinthians 5:17 NKJV). Rahab and her family's statement of faith became exactly this—if old things have passed away, then behold, all things have become new!

What would your statement of faith look like? Think about it and then write it down.

How much do we really know about God and the methods he uses to deal with his children?

How many of his characteristics and traits do you know? Make a list of those you know.

Take time to think, pray and speak your beliefs about God.

Search the Word and make it a point to really know what you believe and why. Then, go and tell others; declare it loud and clear.

When Rahab found herself in a crisis between her people and the men of God, she had to make a very quick decision. For her, it was one that would change her life and her destiny. We, too, will face hard times or situations that need strong but sometimes quick decisions.

One day, a mother and her daughter were in a discussion concerning life's struggles. After preparing three cups of hot water, the mother proceeded to take a carrot, an egg and a coffee bean then place each one into a separate cup. The mother then asked her daughter what she saw. The result was that the heat had turned the carrot soft, the egg hard and the coffee bean had become a wonderful cup of coffee.

Which one are you? Are you like the carrot, going soft and not knowing which way to go? Are you like the egg that starts out soft and willing to listen but then becomes hard-hearted, refusing to bend or compromise? Or, do you work with the trial, not necessarily liking it but listening and compromising when you need to, so that you are like that wonderful cup of coffee?

We must extend God's grace to others, not looking at what we see on the outside, but knowing that God has a plan for them too. Be courageous like Rahab. God will bless you! Try to remember not to tell God how big your storm cloud is but tell that storm cloud how big your God is.

May you have enough happiness to make you sweet, enough trials to make you strong, enough sorrow to keep you human and enough hope to make you happy.

The happiest of people do not necessarily have the best of everything; they just make the most of everything that comes along their way. The brightest future will always be based on a forgotten past; you cannot go forward in life until you let go of your past failures and heartaches. Paul, while writing to the Philippians said, "Actually, I don't have a sense of needing anything personally. I've learned by now to be quite content whatever my circumstances. I am just as happy with little as with much, with much as with little. I have found the recipe for being happy whether full or hungry, hands full or hands empty. Whatever I have, wherever I am, I can make it through anything in the One who makes me who I am" (4:11-13 MSG).

It has been said that when you were born, you were crying and everyone around you was smiling; so live your life in such a way that, at the end, you are the one who is smiling and everyone around you is crying.

James 2:14-17 says, "Dear friends, do you think you'll get anywhere in this if you learn all the right words but never do anything? Does merely talking about faith indicate that a person really has it? For instance, you come upon an old friend dressed in rags and half-starved and say, 'Good morning, friend! Be clothed in Christ! Be filled with the Holy Spirit!' and walk off without providing so much as a coat or a cup of soup—where does that get you? Isn't it obvious that God-talk without God-acts is outrageous nonsense?" (MSG)

Rahab lived the scripture that James spoke of three times, which said, "faith without works is dead" (James 2:14, 20, 26). The message describes it so clearly in James 2:25-26: "The same with Rahab, the Jericho harlot. Was not her action in hiding God's spies and helping them escape—that seamless unity of believing and doing—what counted with God? The very moment you separate body and spirit, you end up with a corpse. Separate faith and works and you get the same thing: a corpse."

Let's Pray

Lord, there is faith and then there is FAITH! Help me to put my faith into action the way Rahab did. Help me not to fear taking a stand for you like she did. You want us to take action and truly care for others, not just in thought but also in action. You want us to bless others as you bless us, and I thank you, Father, for the unexpected blessings you shower on me daily. Help me to put you first and rely on you to take care of the things that I may not understand. You have a plan and purpose for my life and it is one that was decided before I was even born. We are all here for a purpose, Father, and you have a job for each of us to do. It may not seem like much to us, but it may be great to you. I ask that you help me each day to walk hand in hand with you, continuing to do your will here on earth, so that when we meet in heaven you will say, "Well done, faithful servant."

Future Study Scriptures

- Deuteronomy 7: 9
- 1 Samuel 26:23
- Psalm 31:23
- Psalm 36:5
- Psalm 37:3
- Psalm 119:90
- Psalm 89:1
- Isaiah 1:26
- Isaiah 25:1
- Lamentations 3:23
- Hosea 2:20
- Luke 19:17
- 1 Corinthians 1:9

Additional Analysis

For further investigation, read Joshua 2:1-24; 6:17-25

1. The spies were nothing to Rahab; so what prompted her to hide them and lie to the soldiers for them?

2. How do you think Rahab heard and learned so much about God?

3. Why do you think God would use someone like Rahab when someone from a higher or more respected position may have been available?

4. You may know someone who feels like Rahab. What would you say to her to help her to believe that God really wants to forgive her?

5. God tells us not to judge one another. How hard is it, then, to be around those with colourful pasts or whose present behaviour we disagree with?

6. Looking at Rahab's story, what words can we use to describe her character? For example, think of her . . .
   loose past
   knowledge of facts about God
   great act of courage
   confidence in these strangers
   genuine concern for her family's salvation

7. Of all the qualities that we see in Rahab, is there any one to which you can especially relate?

8. Have you ever known anyone with the qualities that you like in Rahab?

9. Why do we still refer to her as "Rahab the prostitute" instead of by what she did or what she became?

10. After what Rahab did for them, why did the spies require an act of obedience from her? Why did they not immediately say that they would protect her house?

11. How does Rahab's life demonstrate the statement that "God loves us too much to leave us where we are"?

12. In the middle of a crisis, how do you react—like a carrot, an egg or a coffee bean?

13. What quality would you like to change in your life? It might seem impossible, but ask God for help and let the Holy Spirit really be in control and guide you. Are you ready to take that step?

Memory Verse

"Your kingdom is built on what is right and fair. Love and truth are in all you do" (Psalm 89:14 NCV).

Newfound Facts

_____

_____

_____

_____

_____

_____

_____

❧ *Then He said to her, "Your sins are forgiven."* ❧

Luke 7:48 (NKJV)

Tears to Liberation

He used the undesirable

(Luke 7:36-50)

I t was party time. Simon was the host and what a host he was! He was a very pompous man who invited Jesus and other Pharisees to come to dinner. There was an elaborate protocol to follow when welcoming special guests, which Simon seemed to have forgotten. In those days, people were either barefoot or in sandals, and it was customary for the host to give water and a towel to his guests to freshen up their very dusty feet. Simon did not do this. It was customary to give a brotherly kiss on the cheek, especially to the guest of honour. Simon missed that one too. He could have placed a drop of oil on the head of Jesus, but no, he did not do that either.

Simon, as a host, where were your manners? Not to worry though, a woman with quite a reputation came to complete the tasks that he forgot. Who, you ask? She was, most likely, the last person Simon thought would ever consider entering his home. You should have heard the gasps of surprise when this woman came into the room. All they could ask was how she dared to come there at that time, for everyone knew that she was such a terrible sinner.

This lady is another one of those women in the Bible whose names we do not know. All we know is that she was a woman with whom a person would not want to be associated. The Amplified Bible calls her "an especially wicked sinner." She was a notorious sinner, a social outcast devoted to sin. From this description of her, it is not difficult to gather that the people did not like her and that they considered her to be a very bad person. At that moment, she did not care what others thought or how it looked, though, because she had set her eyes on serving and honouring Jesus. Through her actions, God used her to reach out to the other guests at that dinner.

As all of the guests are reclining, this woman comes out of the crowd, carrying an alabaster box. Her face is tense, showing the pain of her lifetime, and her eyes are welling up with tears. The host, Simon, and the others send piercing and icy scowls her way, trying to get her to leave before she reaches this very special guest. Even though some of the guests may have desired to visit her later, they do not want to see her now, not there.

Disturbed at what is taking place, Simon continues to watch as she makes her way right up to the guest of honour, Jesus. Wishing she would just disappear, but not wanting to cause a scene, Simon can only watch as she moves forward. What is she doing? She kneels at the feet of Jesus and touches his feet. She is unclean, and the unclean should never touch the clean. In his mind, Simon must have been screaming at her, "Stop it! Just go away!" Okay, fine, Jesus will recognize her for what she is and he will tell her to stop and to go away.

Can you imagine the shock for Simon when Jesus does not rebuke her? He just lets her continue. Now she is weeping and her tears are falling freely. She is crying so much and so hard that her tears are bathing Jesus' feet. What now? She is taking her hair down! Women are not supposed to have their hair down in public, but this woman does not care. She continues to ignore those around her and dries his feet gently with her long, soft hair. This woman is there on a mission—to show love to Jesus. She has come with a humble heart and her alabaster box. She has come with a sacrifice of faith and honour for Jesus. Continuing, she smothers his feet with kisses like we kiss a newborn baby.

The final straw is when she takes the valuable perfume from the alabaster box and pours it over Christ's feet. At this point, Simon must have been fuming inside, thinking, "How dare this woman do this? Who does she think she is? She is ruining my celebration. She is nothing but a harlot, one to be used by men, not honoured and valued."

Have you ever been deep in thought, only to discover that the person beside you seemed to know just what it was that you were thinking? They say that twins are often like this, and I know that my daughters, who are not twins but have felt this way. At one point, one of them was in Europe and needed something, and her sister, who was in Canada, knew that she was going to call and ask for it before the phone rang. We call it bizarre, but God knows everything, so it is not bizarre for him.

Several times throughout the Bible, it says that God knows our very thoughts without us even speaking. This was the case for Simon, and, without Simon even saying one word, Jesus looked at him and began a very weighty conversation and a hearty lesson.

Jesus told a story to Simon, "'There was a certain creditor who had two debtors. One owed five hundred denarii, and the other fifty. And when they had nothing with which to repay, he freely forgave them both. Tell Me, therefore, which of them will love him more?' Simon answered and said, 'I suppose the one whom he forgave more'" (Luke 7:41-43). Then Jesus rebuked Simon, his host. "When I entered your home you gave me no water to wash my feet but this woman has washed my feet with her tears and dried them with her own hair. You did not give me a kiss on the cheek even though I was the honored guest and this woman has not stopped kissing my feet. Finally, you did not anoint my head with oil and this woman has poured expensive fragrant perfume over my feet" (v. 44-46 NKJV). Oh, the embarrassment and anger that must have stormed through Simon—Jesus had rebuked him, and if that was not bad enough, it was in front of all of his friends.

This woman used four ways to show her tremendous love for Jesus and to further demonstrate her total submission and obedience to him. She washed his feet, she dried them with her hair, she kissed them and she anointed them with perfume. She used this event as a form of great worship for the King of Kings. She showed him respect and dignity as she acknowledged her own self-unworthiness.

But is this where Jesus ends their interaction? No, not on your life! He goes on to forgive this woman, this harlot, this sinner, this reject from society. Luke 7:48 says "Then He said to her, 'Your sins are forgiven'" (NKJV). He has just forgiven her of ALL her sins, even though he declared that they were many. He forgave her and paid her debt; the sinful woman was sinful no more, and a new clean woman stood before them!

Jesus, what are you doing?

All of Simon's guests were thinking, "Who is this man who says he can forgive sins? How can he do that, for not even the priests declare sins forgiven? Only God has the authority to forgive sin!" The room must have grown quiet as the tension grew and the guests' conversation dropped to whispers. The loudest sound would have been the cries of this woman, which were even louder now. She thought that she was in a downward spiral, but Jesus reached in and pulled her to the top and out of the pit. The joy of the forgiveness that she received from Jesus must have completely overwhelmed her. She was probably praising God verbally, not just under her breath. As outspoken as she may have been, Simon found himself just the opposite—completely dumbfounded by what had just taken place.

This woman's boldness helped to set her free. She is the one who took the initial step by coming to this event, and she is the one who moved through the crowd with her alabaster box to get a little closer to Jesus. When she found him at last, she was standing behind him with tears rolling down her face. The Holy Spirit touched her heart and she had to move forward; she had to get to Jesus and wash his dusty feet. She had to demonstrate her prayer, asking for his mercy on her life. She could not stop crying, and there were so many tears that there was enough moisture to wash his feet completely. From there, she just could not stop until she completed her task. Jesus knew her for what she really was—a child of the Almighty God. Society only saw her as just another sinful woman, but Jesus touched her inside and out that very night and transformed her into a new creation.

Turn Your Heart

This woman showed Jesus that she loved him and was willing to humble herself before him and to beg for his mercy. We may not like to admit that we have sin in our lives, but we must. Thank God that he does not leave us in our sinful state because, like this woman, we can hear those sweet words, "Your sins are forgiven." All we must do is come to him with a heart of repentance and humility and ask him for his mercy and grace. We are all debtors with a debt that we cannot begin to repay. We have found ourselves sold into sin since the time of Adam and Eve.

I remember people telling me when I was a child that my soul was marked with the original sin of Adam and Eve as soon as I was born. They continued to say that, through baptism, the mark would lighten, but there was no way I could ever completely eradicate it. A shadow of the mark would remain forever as a reminder of what took place in the Garden of Eden. How bleak that sounds, but how liberating it is to realize that Jesus is waiting for you with open arms, ready to erase all sin and make your soul as white as freshly fallen snow. Isaiah 1:18 tells us: "Come now let's reason together Says the lord, Though your sins are like scarlet, they shall be made white as snow; though they are like crimson, they shall be white as wool."

The devil may be waiting in the wings, holding a large credit card ready to increase our debt limit at any time, but he does not own the bank. God does! On judgment day, the devil will not be there to settle the accounts. It will be God. The wages of sin is death, BUT Jesus has repaid those wages and claimed us as his. God is waiting to forgive you and change you by his Holy Spirit. Will you come now?

Let's Pray

Thank you, Jesus, your love for me is so great that even my sins cannot keep me from you. Lord, when others rejected me, you were there to accept me. When I rejected myself, you were there to declare that you love and forgive me. You are the one who rallies beside me and helps me to see and overcome my greatest fears.

"Into the sea of forgetfulness you've placed all of my sins. I'm the one who keeps reminding you over and over again." I thank you, God, that I can be bold enough to bring my sins and lay them at your feet, and that you are waiting to pick them up and tell me those sweet words, "You are forgiven." Help me to continually look to you to keep my path straight and focused. Keep me ready to accept your forgiveness without trying to constantly berate myself for the sins you have already forgiven. But if I fall, may I have the courage to once again look up to see your wonderful face, know your love and feel the blessing of your forgiveness.

Future Study Scriptures

- Psalm 27:13
- Psalm 119:176
- Ezekiel 34:16
- Matthew 10:6
- Matthew 18:11
- Matthew 26:6–13
- Luke 9:25
- Luke 14:34
- Luke 19:10
- Luke 15:6
- Luke 15:24

Additional Analysis

For further investigation, read Luke 7:36-50

1. Simon knew well the customs required each time a special guest entered his home. Why do you think he forgot or chose to ignore them when Jesus was his guest?

2. The woman went straight for Jesus when she entered the room, not speaking to anyone. Name two reasons why she might have been so focused.

3. What do you think she was really looking for when she came? For example, was it for forgiveness, attention or even just a chance to say "I love you"?

4. Has there ever been a time when you just could not find any words to say because you were overwhelmed with emotion? Did you continue in the situation or did you back away? Describe.

5. Make a list of some of the emotions that might have engulfed this woman.

6. What were the four steps she followed as she met Jesus?

7. What would the Pharisees have been thinking of her and of Jesus when he did not send her away like they thought he would?

8. Think of a time when you were reprimanded by someone like Simon was. How did it make you feel: embarrassed, sad or angry? How did you react to the words—did you fight back, say nothing and walk away or feel resentful? How do you think we should react?

9. What do you think took place at the celebration after this woman's encounter with Jesus?

10. Do you think this woman returned to being just another sinful woman, or did she change and become a follower and witness for Jesus and his love?

11. Have you ever had the same experience as this sinful woman, where everyone avoided you unless it was on their terms and in their timing? What did your acquaintances do to act like the Pharisees? Did even one person come and show the love and kindness of Jesus to you?

12. We may think of worship as singing songs in church, but there are many other ways to worship God. Read the following verses and then describe other methods of worship that are noted: Psalm 29:2, Psalm 95:6, Psalm 99:5

13. What valuable lessons have you learned from this woman, a sinner who was made clean?

Memory Verse

"Sing praise to the Lord, because he has done great things. Let all the world know what he has down" (Isaiah 12:5 NCV).

Newfound Facts

_____

_____

_____

_____

_____

_____

_____

_____

_____

_____

_____

_____

⁓ But now, O LORD You are our Father; we are the clay, and you our potter; and we are the work of Your hand ⁓

Isaiah 64:8 (NKJV)

13

Looking to the Future

He can use you . . .

Will you let Him?

We have now seen deep into the lives of several biblical women and discovered what God did through them. God has revealed to us that status has no place in his kingdom. He can and will use people whom we may see as ordinary and unlikely.

Two factors that most of the women had in common are faith and trust in God. No matter what they had gone through or were going through, they trusted that God could do what he said he would do. Some of these women lived in places full of pagan worship, but somehow they heard and knew that the God of Israel was real. Some of them tried to go their own course and failed, but our loving God was waiting and ready to restore them.

The second common denominator is that several of the women whom we have studied remain nameless. I find this very significant because it says to all of us that we do not have to be a "somebody" for God to move through us. He can use people whom we consider ordinary. All we must do is remain willing and ready to participate.

Do you ever feel ordinary? I know I do, and sometimes I wonder and ask God—why me? Why do you want to use me? Wouldn't someone else with more influence or more education be more effective? God does not care who we are, just where our hearts are. Throughout time, God has been looking for women who have agreeable hearts, regardless of whether they do not appear to be perfect. We have seen what he did in biblical times, and, since then, he has also worked through ordinary and unlikely women throughout history.

What do you think of if I say the name Barbra Streisand? Success and riches come to mind, but it was not always that way for her. Barbra was born in 1942, during the Second World War and not many years after the Depression. Times were still hard. Her father passed away when she was only 15 months old, and she never really got along with her stepfather. She started her career as an actress a long way from the lights of Broadway, where we might imagine seeing her today. The theatres were very small, few people came and the pay was very minimal. She continued working there until her boyfriend at the time offered to help her to develop a club act that she initially performed in a gay bar. Her very own mother told her to give up because she would never make it—she was too ugly, had no talent and could not sing. When I first read this I laughed, knowing where she is now. She knew that she could make it, and she took the attitude "I will show them!" As well as being an actress/singer/director, she is a composer/ producer/designer/author/ photographer/activist. She has a long list of accomplishments. She is the only artist to ever receive Oscar, Tony, Emmy, Grammy, Directors Guild of America, Golden Globe, National Medal of Arts and Peabody Awards, as well as France's Legion d'Honneur and the American Film Institute's Lifetime Achievement Award. She is also the first female film director to receive the Kennedy Center Honors.

They say that dreams come true for all who wait—or do they? Jennifer Rothschild, like so many of us in junior high school, had a dream of a future career. She had aspirations of becoming a commercial artist and cartoonist. Every chance she got, she would get a nice, crisp white piece of paper from her dad's office and try to draw characters as well and as quickly as she could. Little did she know that her dreams and plans were going to come crashing down and that she would have to stop drawing forever. In 1979, while Jennifer was in grade nine, she realized that she was not seeing what those around her did. She would bump into other students as they changed classes, see "3"s for "8"s in math class and miss the ball when playing a friendly game of baseball.

What could be wrong? She carried her concerns alone until finally she couldn't deal with it any longer and had to tell her parents. The first reaction of the local ophthalmologist was to give her stronger glasses. When that didn't work, she was sent to Bascom Palmer Eye Institute where they were able to discover the root of the problem. Jennifer had a form of retinitis pigmentosa, which meant that her retinas were disintegrating and there was no known treatment or cure. It was inevitable that her sight would completely disappear, leaving her to discover a new world—a world of darkness.

By the time she graduated from high school, Jennifer had completely lost her sight. Yet, even this new set of circumstances could not hold her back. Jennifer not only finished high school but went on to complete her university degree. To top it off, Jennifer was crowned the homecoming queen for both.

That wasn't the end of Jennifer's story of success but rather only the beginning. For the past 25 years, she has replaced her hunger for drawing with music and sharing the Word of God. While speaking, she strategically tells no-nonsense stories filled with humour, images and messages of hope and encouragement that you can use in your everyday life. Several weekends throughout the year, you will find Jennifer, with her husband at her side, sharing her message with women around the country. Jennifer may have lost her sight but not her love for women and for God. She has joined Beth Moore to lead women's conferences in addition to many other speaking engagements, including Women of Faith. Jennifer has been featured on television productions, including a Billy Graham telecast, Focus on the family, Dr. Phil and many others. She has been the featured cover story in many magazines including *Today's Christian Woman*. Besides these and many other appearances, she is the founder and publisher of a very popular online magazine WOMENSMINISTRY.NET and is the author of over five books and bible studies. One of Jennifer's books is called *Lessons I Have Learned in the Dark*, but listening to her, you will see the light of God and how he wants to direct the plans and purposes of our lives.

Thelma Wells is a woman of whom you may never have heard, but let me tell you about her. She was born in the south to a young woman who was not only unwed but also disabled. Unable to care for her new baby, Thelma was raised by her great-grandparents, who were very loving and made sure that she had a strong Christian upbringing. On the other hand, when she spent time with her maternal grandparents, it was a different story. Her maternal grandmother did not share that same love. This grandma felt embarrassed by her own daughter's physical disability and the fact that Thelma was born out of wedlock. To top it off, she felt that Thelma was too dark-skinned, too black. If her husband, who loved Thelma, did not take her with him whenever he left the house, Grandma Dot would hustle her into a very narrow, dark and insect-infested closet and close the door. Thelma tried to remain brave and would pass the long hours by singing Sunday school songs like "Jesus Loves Me! This I Know," continuing to sing until she would fall asleep. God heard those prayers and rewarded her with his peace and joy, all the while protecting her from developing feelings of anger or bitterness toward her grandma.

When she graduated from high school, Thelma wanted to continue her education and go to secretarial school. She spoke to the school over the phone and was invited to come right down and register. When she walked into the school and informed them about why she was there, she was in for a disappointing surprise. The person behind the desk said sharply, "Oh no you don't! No black person has ever entered our school, and none ever will." This was so surprising, especially since this was after the Rosa Parks incident. You may remember that she was the lady who refused to go to the back of the bus, which is where all black people were made to sit. The front of the bus was only for white people. She is another everyday person who was used in a mighty way, but that is another story.

Crushed, but determined not to give up, Thelma found God opening doors for her, and she ended up going to college. She continued to blaze trails for other black women and all women. As a student at North Texas State University in Denton, Texas (now the University of North Texas), she completed her bachelor's degree and was among the first set of girls to integrate the school's dormitory. At age 61, she received a

Master's of Ministry from the Master's International School of Divinity in Evansville, Indiana, where she became the school's first black female professor. Over the years, many other doors have opened for her: she has been a banker, taught banking, become a successful author and spoken to thousands of women around the world. For many years, Thelma spoke at the Women of Faith Conferences that have already reached out to well over one million women.

Even with this busy schedule, Thelma makes time for her husband, George Wells; her three children; nine grandchildren; and three great grandchildren (for now). To her friends, she is lovingly known as "Mamma T."

Who would have thought that an illegitimate child with nothing to her name would become such an amazing and successful woman of faith, sharing God all over the world? Thelma lives by the motto "In Christ, I can Bee the Best I can Bee!" She believes it to be of encouragement to her and to others. Why, you ask? Thelma explains that scientifically, the bumblebee should not even be able to fly. Its body is too big and its wingspan too narrow. Yet, it ignores all the laws of aeronautical science and flies around doing its job just as God wants it to do. Many times, I've heard her give her statement of affirmation that says that God thought it and planned it and, because he uses ordinary people, he can do it.

Okay, so these women have gone through hardships and God has worked through them; but he cannot want everyone, can he? You might think, "How can God use me after where I have been and all that I have done?" Let us look at another woman who was not such a good girl. In fact, she called herself a really bad girl.

Liz Curtis Higgs came from a family in small-town USA. Her parents tried to keep their daughter on the straight and narrow, but Liz, like so many others, thought she knew best how to run her own life. As a teenager, she started stealing smokes from her mom's purse and then moved on to skipping school so that she could smoke pot. By the time she was 20, she was spending four to five nights each week in the bar drinking and trying to find Mr. Right. She worked at a radio station and was so bad that Howard Stern—himself noted for his excessive use of vulgar language—once told her that she would have to clean up her act. By 1981, she was using pot, speed, cocaine and alcohol, leading a very loose lifestyle when it came to men and heading down a path that could only lead to doom and destruction.

But remember, God loves us too much to leave us where we are, and that included Liz Curtis Higgs. She left New York and moved to work at a radio station in Kentucky where God sent a couple into her life to make friends with her and invite her to church. They never pushed her into church, or even told her that she needed to clean up her life. They did tell her, though, that they believed in her and that God believed in her. They also told her that God had a plan for her life and that Jesus died just for her no matter what kind of life she had been leading. Then they topped if off by telling her that if she would go to church with them, they would buy her lunch. How could she refuse a free lunch? After approximately the seventh time she attended a service, she heard the choir sing "I Have Decided to Follow Jesus." That was it—the Holy Spirit got hold of her, she went straight up to the baptistery and a new life began.

Today, Liz is a very accomplished speaker who has shared her words of love and encouragement throughout the USA as well as 11 other countries. Since 1986, she has presented well over 1,600 very inspirational programs. She was awarded the Council of Peers Award for Excellence, and is one of only approximately 40 women in the world to ever be named to the Speaker Hall of Fame by the National Speakers Association. On top of this, she has reached hundreds of thousands of people with her books, including several for children, as well as her videos and tapes. Each of her 28 books, several of which are award-winning, tells a story of mercy, forgiveness and encouragement.

Even with someone who was following a path of such doom and destruction, God was able to change it all. Like Liz, all we need to do is follow the words of the song and say, "I have decided to follow Jesus." He can take us off that doomed highway and place us on a path to success and a new life.

For Liz, God was with her and helped her to meet her husband. They met at a friend's wedding—yes, in a church. Liz married Bill, who was a broadcasting engineer with a Ph.D. in Old Testament languages; he was also two years her senior. Today, Bill is Liz's director of operations for her speaking office. Bill and Liz have two grown children, Matthew and Lillian, who have graduated from college. God worked through and in Liz Curtis Higgs and turned her into a strong woman who carries the label "encourager."

The final modern-day woman I want to examine is Mother Teresa, a wonderful lady about whom we have all heard; but most know so little about her, apart from her exceptional work in India. On August 26, 1910, in Skopje (also known as Uskup), a town in the Turkish Empire and capital of the Republic of Macedonia, Agnes Gonxha Bojaxhiu was born. She was from a family that people considered very well-off. Her father was in construction, so money was not a problem for part of her young life. In an instant, her life changed when her father died suddenly and her mother became the sole caretaker of the three children.

Aga, as she was called, was always very fascinated with stories of missionary life and service. If you gave her a map, she could pinpoint where there were missions and tell you the services that were being supplied in each place. In 1928, at the age of 18, she decided to become a nun. She chose to go to Ireland, which was far from her family and the only life she had ever known. It sounds a little like Sarah, who we read left everything she knew to follow her husband Abraham. While Aga was there, she was described as "very small, quiet and shy," and another person called her "ordinary." A year later, she went to a girls' school in Calcutta, India, the city where she would live the rest of her life. She was sheltered in the convent, teaching young girls until 1946, when God opened her eyes to see the beggars, lepers and the homeless. She also saw the unwanted infants left to die on the streets and in garbage bins. God's tug on her heart made her leave the protection of the young girls' school and move out to care for these needy people in the slums of Calcutta.

This assignment began with just her and God—but not for long. Many of those who came to help her were former students from the same girls' school at which she had taught earlier. Each new recruit who came had to take a vow of poverty with her. They were not to accept any material reward for their work. In October of 1950, Mother Teresa received permission to begin a new order of nuns, "The Missionaries of Charity." Pope Paul VI granted her organization the status of International Religious Family in 1965.

God worked through Mother Teresa to accomplish things that we would think were impossible. She convinced the Indian government to give her a portion of an abandoned temple dedicated to the Hindu goddess of death and destruction. She turned it into a home to care for those on the streets who were dying. This matched the mission that she had for the order of nuns, which was to demonstrate God's love and care to those whom nobody else would even look at, let alone take care of. Her list of accomplishments is great, including receiving a Nobel Peace Prize in 1971, along with several other worldwide honour awards. Because of Mother Theresa and her work, nuns and priests are reaching people in countries all over the world in the name of the order that she founded. When there are catastrophes, such as floods, famine and epidemics, they ignore their own needs in order to take care of others. They also work daily with shut-ins, the homeless and those suffering from alcoholism and AIDS.

Even so, the one thing that people remember about her is that, throughout her lifetime, she remained extremely humble. It is said that when she passed away, all she owned was her shawl and her Bible; but still, she felt that she had lived a very rich life. This woman may have only been about five feet tall at her best, but she was a powerhouse whom God used to reach the world, a woman who, instead of going from rags to riches, went from riches to work with those in rags.

None of these women stood out as special to the world when they were children, but God had a plan and a purpose for each of them. He wanted to help them to move mountains, and they have and continue to do so. God wants you to open yourself to him and say, "Here I am; use me as you will." We need to stop thinking that there is no way; there IS a way when we look to God for help. With him, nothing can stop us.

Mother Teresa once said, "I alone cannot change the world, but I can cast a stone across the waters to create many ripples."

In the 60s, Helen Reddy sang "I am woman, hear me roar!" We are women; hear us roar for the work that God has prepared for us to do! God created our tasks in his great plan before we were even a twinkle in our parents' eyes. Jeremiah 1:5 tells us loud and clear; "Before I shaped you in the womb, I knew all about you. Before you saw the light of day, I had holy plans for you" (MSG). Tasks were not created *because* we were born—God had a plan prepared before we were even born, and now it is time to allow him to work through us and in us to complete that plan.

As I have said before, I would never have believed that God would have given me a passion for women like he has. I never thought in a million years that I would be able to minister to women and encourage them. If you looked at my adolescent list of potential professions, ministry was not even on it. I thought that I wanted to be a probation officer, and then I discovered sales and really enjoyed it for a season. I finally ended up with my fund-raising management career, only to have it end unexpectedly and the door to ministry open wide. Now, this did not happen overnight, but I needed to keep myself open to what God wanted. I believe that we are all tools in the hands of the Lord and that he wants to cultivate his garden using us however and wherever he needs. I want to be a useful tool, not one left in the garden shed because it does not work. How about you?

Are you willing to say right now, "Here I am, Jesus, use me in ANY way that you desire?" You may see yourself as plain and ordinary, but God sees you as beautiful, special and necessary for the advancement of his kingdom. He sees you as one who can help lead others into a relationship with Jesus, whether by planting a seed, laying down fertilizer, cultivating the soil or harvesting. We all need to see and accept ourselves in the words of this following letter, which is based on scripture:

Dear Father God in heaven,

Before you shaped me in my mother's womb, you knew all about me. Before I saw my first light of day, you had holy plans for me.
Jeremiah 1:5

You know me inside and out, you know every bone in my entire body.
Psalm 139:13

You pay attention to me, down to the last detail—even numbering the very hairs on my head.
Matthew 10:30

You created me as a human being; you created me to be god-like.
Genesis 1:27

Starting from scratch, you made the entire human race and made the earth hospitable, with plenty of time and space for living, so we could seek after you and not just grope around in the dark, but also actually find you.
Acts 10:26

I am an open book to you; even from a distance, you know what I am thinking.
Psalm 139:1

You know when I leave and when I get back; I am never out of your sight.
Psalm 139:2

You know everything I am going to say before I even start the sentence.
Psalm 139:7

We have to remember that we are your temple and that you are present in each of us. No one can get out of your sight to vandalize your temple, we can be sure of that.
1 Corinthians 3:16-17

God, you are a safe place to hide, ready to help when I need you.
Psalm 46:1

God, you made my life complete when I placed all the pieces before you. When I got my act together, you gave me a fresh start . . . . I feel put back together and I am watching my step.
Psalm 18:20-22

Is there any like you, God? Who is a rock, except you? Is it not you who armed me then aimed me in the right direction?
Psalm 18:31

God, you can do anything—far more than we could ever imagine, guess or request in our wildest dreams! You do it, not by pushing us around, but by sending your Spirit to work deeply and gently within us.
Ephesians 3:20

God, your various ministries can be carried out everywhere, but they originate in your Spirit. Your various expressions of power are in action everywhere, but you are behind it all. We are all given something to do that shows others who you are. Everyone gets in on it and everyone benefits. The variety is wonderful!
1Corinthians 12:4-7

We neither make nor save ourselves. You do both the making and the saving. You created each of us to join Christ Jesus in the work he does and the good work that he prepared for us to do—work you say we had better be doing.
Ephesians 2:10

God is love. When we take up permanent residence in the life of love, we live in you and you live in us.
1 John4: 17

Light, space, zest—that is you, God! So, with you on my side I am fearless, afraid of no one and nothing!
Psalm 27:1

Love,
Your Daughter

Turn Your Heart

Ladies, this is it. The time is now and we need to follow the words that Tyrone Williams says as he prays before he ministers: "It's me and you, Holy Spirit, let's do it!"

Well, ladies, let's do it. Let's really turn our lives over to God, and say "Use me, melt me, mould me and fill me." Cry out to Him and say "Spirit of the living God, fall fresh on me!" Here is an exercise that you can try tomorrow morning.

As you get up, thank God for helping you to complete all of the tasks that he has given or will give you for the day.

Just for one day, whatever responsibility you have, do it! Once you have done it, thank God for helping you.

Decide to surround yourself with people who really trust God. A negative person brings a negative message while a positive person is pleasing to your mind and heart.

This is a very basic, but very practical way to grow in godliness. Once you have done it one day, why not try it a second day, and so on?

Let's Pray

We have finished this season of learning about your precious women and how you have used them. Now I ask you, Lord, to use me for your glory and your honour. Thank you, Lord, for what you are doing in my life and how you can use me no matter what my circumstances are or have been, where I am now or where I have been. Bring me to the place that you want me to be, Lord; help me to grow in you and move in you. Help me to realize my value to myself, my family and to you. As we move on, I pray, Lord, for the courage to take a step out of the box and into the world that you have prepared.

Future Study Scriptures

📖 Deuteronomy 2:7	📖 Deuteronomy 30:9
📖 Ruth 2:12	📖 1 Samuel 26:23-25
📖 2 Chronicles 24:13	📖 Job 36:24
📖 Psalm 40:5	📖 Psalm 66:5
📖 Psalm 90:17	📖 Ecclesiastes 3:17
📖 Ecclesiastes 9:1	📖 Ezekiel 29:20
📖 Matthew 6:26	📖 Luke 12-6:8
📖 John 6:28	

Additional Analysis

1. Can you think of a woman whom you have heard of or read about that God has helped along her path like the ones we have just read about? If yes, who is she and how did God use her?

2. In these lessons, what have you learned that can help you? Can you relate to any of the women whom we have discussed? Which ones?

3. Do you accept the fact that God has a plan and purpose for your life?

4. Knowing that we don't get the entire plan at one time, do you think you know any part of that plan? What is it?

5. Search your concordance and find as many scriptures as you can that remind you of God's plan.

6. Are you ready to move out and onward for God?

Okay then, let's do it. Let's be like these women and be bold, strong and hopeful. Be trusting in what God can and will do for you. Let us be ready, peacemakers with determination, eager to use our God-given talents. Be loyal, redeemed and look to the future with anticipation and excitement.

Memory Verse

"We have freedom now, because Christ has made us free" (Galatians 5:1 NCV).

What I have learned

Now it is your turn to take what you have learned here and move onward and outward for the Lord. Remember to study his Word and listen carefully for the direction of the Holy Spirit.

Newfound Facts

_____

_____

_____

_____

_____

_____

_____

_____

_____

Bonus Section
Self or Group Study

*❧ Go therefore and make disciples of all the nations,
baptizing them in the name of the Father and of the Son
and of the Holy Spirit. ❧*

Matthew 28:19 (NKJV)

Getting Started

Let me be the first to welcome you to this eye-opening and challenging study guide. The guide is for women like you who want to grow and learn to walk in the path and the plan that God has for their lives. God has given his word to each of us to help discover the wonderful plan that he has outlined for us.

If you are a bible study leader, we want to make this study fun and easy to follow. The first thing that each person will need is his or her own copy of *One Ordinary Woman One, Extraordinary God*. The second thing every person needs to have is a heart that is open to learning what God has in store for him or her. This can be an exciting journey if you will only let it be.

The following hints will help you if you would like to use this book as an individual or group Bible study.

Time

I find it best to choose a regular time for studying God's Word. Yes, I mean making a daily appointment with God. If I do not plan and set aside a block of time beforehand, I find that the day slips by and I do not spend any time with him at all.

You will have to find the right time of day for you. If you are a morning person, do not plan to spend the time just before bed with God. I know when I first started to study the Bible, I liked to stay up late, but I was trying to read the Word first in the morning and then would fall asleep. All that did was make me feel like a failure.

Choose a reasonable amount of time. If you know that you cannot give an hour at first, then plan for 30 minutes and work up to a longer period. The main point is to prepare. Benjamin Franklin said, "By failing to prepare, you are preparing to fail."

Place

Now that you have found the right time, you need to decide on the right location. Discovering this place can be the biggest challenge of all. When Susanna Wesley, mother of 19 children, including John and Charles Wesley, wanted to spend time with God, she had a unique way of finding her "quiet" place. She would sit down in her kitchen and pull her apron up over her head. Then she would spend time in prayer and her children knew not to disturb her! Can you imagine that? There are two things that Wesley, who was very serious about her faith, felt that everyone must do—*believe* it and *behave* it.

Most of us will not find our kitchen a commotion—or interruption-free zone, but don't give up. Keep searching and trying different areas until you find your perfect spot.

Look for:

- a place in your home where there's not a lot of chaos so you can concentrate on your time with God.

- a place where you are not looking at the inch of dust on the shelf or some other undone chores and thinking about getting them done.

- a place out of hearing range of the kids, husband, telephone, answering machine and/or dog.

- a place away from the TV, radio or computer—and that includes not constantly checking your e-mail. It is too easy to say, "I will just answer this one and then I will start."

Atmosphere

Making the conditions right for you is the third step. If you study best with music playing, then turn the music on. There is documentation that, for many, baroque classical music increases a person's memory retention. If you cannot study with background noise, keep it quiet. You need to use whatever works best for you.

Several years ago, we had a camper that I used to love hiding out in to be completely alone to read and pray. When I entered it alone, I could immediately feel God. This just proves it does not matter where you are, it just matters that you do it. Ask yourself, "How committed am I to getting to know God?" He will always be ready for you no matter the time of day or night. He will never be late for your appointed time. He will never miss it or say that he forgot. He will never say that he is too tired, and he will never be distracted during your time. Can you say the same? It may take time, but keep trying. You will not be sorry!

"But when you pray, go into your room, close the door and pray to your Father, who is unseen. Then your Father, who sees what is done in secret, will reward you." (Matthew 6:6 NIV)

When Did Jesus Pray?

"And when He had sent the multitudes away, He went up on a mountain by Himself to pray. And when evening had come, He was alone there" (Matthew 14:23 NKJV).

"Then Jesus came with them to a place called Gethsemane, and said to the disciples, 'Sit here while I go and pray over there'" (Matthew 26:36 NKJV).

In the early morning: "Now in the morning, having risen a long while before daylight, He went out and departed to a solitary place; and there He prayed" (Mark 1:35).

He prayed often: "So He Himself often withdrew into the wilderness and prayed" (Luke 5:16).

"And it happened, as He was alone praying, that His disciples joined Him, and He asked them, saying, 'Who do the crowds say that I am?'" (Luke 9:18 NKJV).

"And it came to pass, as He was praying in a certain place, when He ceased, that one of His disciples said to Him, 'Lord, teach us to pray, as John also taught his disciples'" (Luke 11:1 NKJV).

He prayed for us: "And I will pray the Father, and He will give you another Helper, that He may abide with you forever" (John 14:16 NKJV).

Where Did Others in the Bible Pray?

"About noon the following day, as they were on their journey and approaching the city, Peter went up on the roof to pray" (Acts 10:9 NIV).

"Now when Daniel learned that the decree had been published, he went home to his upstairs room where the windows opened toward Jerusalem. Three times a day he got down on his knees and prayed, giving thanks to his God, just as he had done before" (Daniel 6:10 NIV).

Bible

My personal Bible is the New King James Version, but I have many others that I reference to get a deeper understanding of what I am reading. Sometimes a different version can also help me to understand what God is saying when I just do not comprehend it in my regular Bible. Some suggestions for translations that you could use include:

For easy reading:

New Century Version (NCV)
Contemporary English Version (CEV)
The Message (MSG)
New Living Translation (NLT)

For study or everyday reading:

New International Version (NIV)
New King James (NKJV)
New American Standard (NASB)

There are also many study or devotional Bibles available. Personally, I use the *Women of Faith* devotional and study Bibles as well as the Cindy Jacobs *Women of Destiny Bible.*

Other Sources of Help:

There are other aids available, but it is not imperative that you go and purchase any of them. Some of these are Bible dictionaries, atlases, concordances and commentaries. There are also Bible search sites available on the Internet that provides this information.

Supplies

Make sure you have all the materials you need. Nothing can distract you more than having to look for a pen that writes, leaving you open to being interrupted by another thing to do before you start again. Have pens, highlighters or other markers in several colors and all materials that you think are necessary. Use a journal and not individual sheets of paper for writing answers, new questions, your thoughts and the thoughts that God shares with you. Writing during your study time is important so that you will remember. Relying on our minds to remember important ideas just does not work. I know. I have tried!

Begin

Now that you have a time, a place, your personal atmosphere and your materials, it is time to begin. I start with praise and prayer, asking God to help me to focus. Without this preparation, I find that when I sit down to study, every possible interruption tries to invade my space. An example of such a prayer might be:

Lord, as I enter the pages of your Word, I need your help to remove any interruptions that try to prevent me from getting closer to you. Please take away the thinking habits I have developed that keep me from hearing your voice and your direction. During this time, help me to discern your voice and your voice alone. As I read your Word, Lord, help me to see the message that you have chosen for me to see. Help me to understand what I am reading rather than just looking at words on a page. Lord, help your Word to become a road map for my life. Also, I need to take your Word and your love and begin to share it with those around me—to practise the great commandment of loving my neighbour as myself. I thank you, Lord, for your help right now. Amen.

When a scripture really speaks to you, write it down and fasten it to your mirror, fridge, closet door or even inside your journal. Try to memorize it so that you can recall it as you need it. "Your word have I hidden in my heart that I may not sin against You" (Psalm 119:11).

You may have to re-read the verse a few times to understand what it means. There is nothing wrong with this, and no, you are not foolish!

The verse may bring up questions other than the ones asked here following each woman's story, and that is wonderful. Write down all of your own questions and then try to answer them yourself or invite some friends to join you.

Check out who wrote the passage that you are reading. Is the story being told in the first person or is it being told by someone else?

There is no absolute right or wrong way to study God's Word. The most important part is that you are doing it. You are reading, which means you are learning. Psalm 119:38 (NKJV) says, "Establish Your word to Your servant, Who is devoted to fearing You." You may want to read all of Psalm 119, as it has many references to learning the Word and then living it.

Have fun! This is a wonderful gift that God has given us to help us in our day-to-day living.

Group Study

A group study is always great because you can hear the thoughts and opinions of others as they respond to the story. Here are some suggestions to help you to prepare for an enjoyable group study experience:

Keep the group size manageable. I believe a maximum size of six to eight people per group allows everyone an opportunity to take part. Otherwise, a quieter person may get lost in the discussion. If you have more people interested in this Bible study, you should begin a second group.

Lay out your group rules before you begin.

There are three rules that I always apply:

1. Anything said in the group stays in the group—some women may share comments that make them very vulnerable and, as leaders, we need to respect that and create an atmosphere with a sense of freedom and safety.

2. No one person should monopolize the discussion.

3. Stay on topic.

    Begin and end the session with praise and prayer. As for individual Bible study, we need to be able to put all of the busyness of the day behind us and focus on God. In order to do that, we need his help and intervention.

A prayer example:

Lord, as we begin our time together to penetrate the pages of your Word, we need your help to remove all thoughts of the day's activities that would prevent us from getting closer to you. Help each of us to keep an open mind to your direction and teaching. Lord, help us to accept each other and help us to learn and grow from each person in this group—from their strengths and their weaknesses. As we read your Word, Lord, help us to see the message that you have chosen for us to see. Help us to understand the words that we read and discuss, that they might not come back empty. Lord, I ask you to reveal yourself to us in this study in the way that you know is best. We ask that you use each of us as your tools to reach out to one another and to those beyond this room. Help us to unite ourselves to your will and your direction. In Jesus' name, we pray, and we thank you in advance for what you are going to do. Amen.

Ask all group members to complete their assigned homework before class so that everyone can take part in the discussion and understand what is going on instead of trying to catch up. Groups will thrive when people share their insights into how the Word has spoken to them.

Just as in school, you need to ensure that you have pens, highlighters and a book in which to write. Try not to use loose pieces of paper as they have a tendency to get lost or misplaced, whereas a book is longer lasting.

Every woman needs to bring her own Bible each week. Within the group, you can expect to have several versions of the Bible and you can read from each one to help people to develop a greater understanding.

Encourage members of the group to keep their own personal journals to document prayers and the answers that come to them. Have the group record scriptures or comments from group members that really speak to them during the study.

To add a little fun, assign a favourite scripture from each of the women studied as a memory verse. Keep track of who remembers them and have a prize for the most scriptures memorized. Rewards are not just for kids!

As a group leader, you need to keep the discussion flowing and on track. Remember, you are there as a facilitator, not a lecturer. You may want to assign a different leader each week to guide the group. This is a great way to develop new leaders. They may be ones who never before realized that they could lead.

Start and end on time. An individual's time is very important and, as the leader, you need to respect that.

Review and use the suggestions given for individual study.

Above all, have fun. Learning should be a joy, not a chore.

As an extra help, I have included a section entitled "Question Notes." This section has answer suggestions for many of that chapter's study questions.

Future Study Scriptures

- Job 22:22
- Job 33:3
- Psalm 138:4
- Proverbs 1:2
- Proverbs 1:7
- Proverbs 4:1
- Proverbs 19:20
- Proverbs 23:12
- Proverbs 24:32
- Jeremiah 20:9
- Jeremiah 32:33
- Jeremiah 36:32
- Ezekiel 3:10
- Luke 8:15
- Romans 10:8
- 1 Corinthians 11:17
- 2 Timothy 3:16

With God guiding you, I know you can do it!

Have fun and make trouble for the devil!

Notes

Question Notes

Never Give Up Hope

Chapter Objective

To know that God has a plan for each of us and that he will give us what we need to know as we need it.

Future Study Focus

God speaks to people in various ways, but no matter what method he selects—dreams, visions, interpretations or other individuals—the fact remains that he will direct us and never leave us. Furthermore, there is nothing too hard for our God, so we can trust him fully.

Questions

1. *Sarah and Sarai mean princess, which suits a mother of nations. Do you know the meaning of your name? If not try to look it up on the Internet or in a baby name book. Do you think the meaning has relevance to your life?*

   Take a baby name book or laptop with Internet access into your class to help those who didn't look up their names to discover the meaning. It can be a fun way to break the ice and it is very interesting to discover how the meaning relates to the person.

   Example: My name, Lorene, means the "laurel" and my husband's name means "crowned with the laurel," so the meaning of my name unquestionably brings merit to my life. To me, it is just another confirmation that we were meant to be together. Laurel was used as a crowning leaf during biblical times and was very significant.

2. *How do you think Sarah felt about herself when it seemed like God would not be giving her a son after he had promised Abraham he would be the father of nations?*

Sarah may have felt that there was something wrong with her or that God was punishing her. When God is silent, sometimes we feel that he has pulled away and that it must be our fault. Sarah may have felt embarrassed and she may have felt like a failure or a disappointment to her husband. God had made the promise to Abraham but never specified that it would be fulfilled with Sarah, which could be why she decided to take charge and design her own plan.

3. *How did Sarah interpret God's silence?*

Sarah, like many of us, did not enjoy exercising patience to calmly wait for the answer; in fact, she found it very annoying. Sarah took God's silence as a sign that she should take charge of the situation and get Abraham a son from someone else.

5. *What was Sarah's reaction when she discovered that her plan was not working as she had designed it?*

Even though it was entirely Sarah's idea for Abraham to be with Hagar, it was easy for her to try to put the blame back onto Abraham when things didn't turn out as she had planned. In that respect, she was like Eve, who ate the fruit, but when God asked her about it, she tried to blame Adam and the snake instead of taking responsibility. Many of us don't like to take ownership of our actions or plans when they don't work out the way that we wanted because we don't want to face the consequences associated with them.

6. *How did her interpretation influence the rest of her life?*

Even after she delivered Isaac, there was no changing the fact that Hagar had Abraham's first son instead of Sarah. She had to live with Hagar's comments and suffer the animosity that developed between them. Sarah became very mean-spirited toward Hagar instead of getting along with her as they had done prior to the pregnancy. Her plan robbed her of the joy that she would have felt while pregnant with her first child.

7. *Sarah laughed at the announcement that she was going to have a baby. How do you think you would have reacted?*

Sarah's reaction probably seems mild compared to the laughter and complete disbelief that there would be if it were happening today. After 50, a woman expects a life of no children except for grandchildren. Therefore, at over 90, many women today would question God as to what he was doing, and most would not rejoice in it. There was a woman in Italy who delivered a child in her early sixties and it made the world news—can you imagine if she were 90 what the media would have to say about that?

8. *What emotions may Sarah have experienced when she discovered that she was pregnant?*

There would have been several emotions running through Sarah's heart. She would have felt excited that she would finally give Abraham a child. She probably wished it could have been earlier. She may have wondered how she would ever be able to take care of a child when she herself was getting weaker and very tired. She may have even felt some regret for not trusting God enough to follow through with his plan and for the fact that now this was Abraham's second son, not his first.

9. *What do you think was the biggest test of Sarah's faith?*

It may be helpful to recognize that there were actually two substantial tests of faith for Sarah in this process. The first involved waiting for God to fulfill his plan for her husband. He had made a promise that Abraham would be the father of nations but did not say who would be the mother. You would assume, since she was Abraham's wife, that it would be her, but maybe, through lack of trust, she questioned God. The result was that she didn't do well with this test and had Hagar enter the picture. The second test of faith was when she finally did get pregnant. She had to trust that God would take care of her and make her able to take care of her child at her age.

The underlying component of Sarah's tests was to see if she had trust and faith that God would do what he said he would do. However, in order to pass, she also needed a dose of patience.

10. *What evidence is there that she experienced real low points?*

Sarah's lowest point must have been when she honestly felt that she would never have the child that God promised to Abraham. When people are suffering from depression, they don't always see things clearly and can act irrationally, which is what Sarah did. She stopped trusting God and started to play the "What if?" game. If I just do this one thing—then at least Abraham will be happy and fulfilled. In Sarah's lifetime, if a woman could not give her husband a child within five years of marriage, it was considered very normal for her to give her husband one of the servants to sleep with. Sarah had to think of reasons that seemed logical to her to encourage Abraham to sleep with Hagar.

Another low point in Sarah's life was after the birth of Ishmael. Hagar and Ishmael rubbed her face in the fact that she could not give her husband the son that God promised, generally causing dissention in their family and stress for Sarah.

12. *Find and list here at least five other scriptures that tell us not to fear. What do these scriptures tell us about God?*

Genesis 21:17 "And God heard the voice of the lad. Then the angel of God called to Hagar out of heaven, and said to her, 'What ails you, Hagar? **Fear not,** for God has heard the voice of the lad where he is.'"

Genesis 26:24 "And the LORD appeared to him the same night and said, 'I am the God of your father Abraham; **do not fear,** for I am with you. I will bless you and multiply your descendants for My servant Abraham's sake.'"

Genesis 35:17 "Now it came to pass, when she was in hard labour, that the midwife said to her, '**Do not fear**; you will have this son also.'"

Genesis 46:3 "So He said, 'I am God, the God of your father; **do not fear** to go down to Egypt, for I will make of you a great nation there.'"

Ruth 3:11 "And now, my daughter, **do not fear**. I will do for you all that you request, for all the people of my town know that you are a virtuous woman."

As it says in Philippians 4:13 (NKJV), "I can do all things through Christ who strengthens me." The important thing to remember is that the word "God" and the word "trust" go hand in hand. Yes, God is love, but if we don't trust him, then we won't be able to accept his love. God is full of mercy and grace, but without trusting him, we won't be able to believe that his mercy and grace won't be taken away from us if we fall. Failing to accept his goodness and love will result in an invisible but very strong wall being erected, blocking all that he wants to pour out onto us.

On the other hand, when we trust God, we know that he wants the best for us and if he asks us to do it, he will be there to give us the strength to see it to completion. We have to keep our eyes focused on him, even on what we think may be impossible, for God says, "I am with you and you can and will do it."

❷

Loving and Trusting

Chapter Objective

The discussion of Mary's life encourages us to love and not be afraid. God will not ask us to do anything that we are unable to do, nor will he leave us alone after he asks.

Future Study Focus

God is love and we are to love him and keep his commandments. It is impossible to show love to God and do our own thing at the same time. We must make a choice.

Questions

1. *Many of us have had special people influence our lives. What does being a role model mean to you? Who are your role models? Are any of them teens or much younger than you are?*

The American Psychological Association defines a role model as a person who serves as an example of the values, attitudes and behaviours associated with a role. For example, a father is a role model for his sons. Role models can also be people who distinguish themselves in such a way that others admire and want to emulate them. A woman who becomes a successful brain surgeon or airline pilot can be described as a role model for other women. I think this also outlines what being a role model should be like for a Christian woman. Our goal should be to have people see us and want what we have as we emulate the love of God. If they haven't already chosen him as their Lord and Saviour, it should be our aspiration to have them want to do so.

Several role models in my Christian walk have influenced me in one way or another. One young person I can think of is a young man who was in my Sunday school class. When this young fellow prayed, it would bring tears to my eyes because of his passion and his belief and expectation for an answer. One week he prayed for his dad to get a job and the next week he bounced in and asked if he could share. With excitement, he told how God had answered his prayers and that his dad was now working. We all need to have this kind of trust and belief.

5. *From Mary's reaction, what do we see about her relationship with God?*

Mary had a very deep and all-encompassing relationship with God that she obviously developed from a God-centred upbringing. She showed an honest assessment of herself and her lifestyle and came up with true humility, desiring a very authentic relationship with God. From the love that she felt toward God, she demonstrates how we should react when he calls. Because of her love and respect for God, if he needed her she wanted to be there and ready without hesitation whenever he called.

7. *What outcomes can we generate for ourselves by not believing in God's promises?*

None of us intentionally goes out and searches for second best, so why are we willing to accept it from God? God wants to pour out his blessings on us but our unbelief erects a huge wall to stop them. We may also find ourselves out of his will, which is not where we want to be. This place never brings joy or comfort—only struggles and unhappiness.

8. *Mary's life changed drastically after her response to God. In what ways do you see it becoming harder?*

Before her acceptance, she was just Mary, a young girl in the village. After she returned from Elizabeth's she would have been unable to hide her pregnancy and would have heard the whispers and felt the cold stares due to her being pregnant and unmarried. She would have been looked upon and labelled a loose woman. Until Joseph heard from the angel, she knew that he could and possibly would cancel their marriage and that she would always be looked at as damaged.

In addition, she was young and now was not just a mother but the mother of Jesus, whom she knew would not stay with her forever because he was the son of God. She would always be wondering when God would take him to finish his mission, even while she was experiencing the feelings of being a mother who loved her son and would not want to lose him. As Jesus grew, she would have felt joy as he performed miracles and told of God's love, completing the work of his Father, but on the other hand, she also felt the enormous pain that people inflicted upon him, as she had to stand back and watch them torture and kill her son. She must have been inconsolable.

10. *Why do you think God selected Mary to be the mother of Christ? After all, she was young, inexperienced and not very well off.*

God wanted to show the world that it doesn't matter where we are in life or what we have; he can use us if we are well-intentioned. Mary was very young but God demonstrated that no matter what age we are, he can use us if we are willing. Mary is referred to as "average," so if average is how we see ourselves, Jesus can use us because he came from someone just like us.

When Jesus was taken to the temple for purification, the Bible points out that Mary and Joseph were not wealthy. It was the custom to bring a lamb and two doves, but Leviticus 12:8 tells us that those who couldn't afford to bring a lamb were to bring two doves or two pigeons—one for a burnt offering and one for a sin offering. Mary and Joseph only brought two doves, demonstrating their low income. Knowing this prevents anyone from saying that he or she is too poor to be used by God.

③

A Lifelong Mission

Chapter Objective

God has a place for each of us in his great plan and we need to trust him to know what is the best way and time to pursue it. In turn, we need to do our best to constantly praise him along the way.

Future Study Focus

God will show mercy and forgive us when we mess up. It is our duty and honour to spend time praising him for everything he does.

Questions

2. *What characteristics or personality traits do you see in Miriam?*

—She was a **watchwoman.** She demonstrated the need to be on your toes and ready for when God calls you to something, whatever it may be.

—She was very **protective.** She watched over her brother as he was placed in the reeds as an infant.

—She was a **leader.** She demonstrated this when she led the people in worship after they crossed the Red Sea.

—She was a **counsellor**. She was there for her brother Moses to talk with, which would have been very unusual for a woman in that day.

—She was **competitive**. She questioned her brother's leadership.

—She was a **witness for God**. She worshipped and obeyed him most of the time, and after she recovered from the week of leprosy, she knew why she had been afflicted and she knew who healed her, which would have made her even more of a witness.

—She was called a **prophetess**. Scripture doesn't record any of Miriam's specific words of prophesy as we know it, but praise and dancing was taught to the prophets as part of their role.

3. *How important was Miriam's role in her brother's future?*

For the most part, Miriam was there for Moses, or you could say that she "had his back." The Bible tells us how, as a child and as an older sister, Miriam helped her mother Jocabed to hide Moses to prevent him from being put to death (Exodus 1:22). When he was placed in the reeds, Miriam stayed back and watched over him. Then, still watching out for his best interest, after watching Pharaoh's daughter find him, she stepped forward to quickly suggest that she could find a nursemaid for this child (Exodus 2:7-10).

When Moses led the people out of Egypt, Miriam was there. As they crossed the Red Sea and witnessed the miracle of the armies being defeated, she led the dance and singing following the prayer from Moses. She travelled beside them as they wandered through the wilderness. She was with Moses each time the Israelites got their backs up and tried to turn from God and oppose Moses. She was there as, each time, they went back looking for mercy through hunger, thirst and disease. She was there when Moses came back down the mountain with the commandments. She saw the tabernacle built and watched as Aaron was made a high priest.

She repeatedly saw how God used Moses as his representative. She may not have been front and centre through all of these events, but she was his big sister and a prophetess (Exodus15:20) who God used as a leader for the people. In the book of Micah, we also read, "I sent Moses to lead you, also Aaron and Miriam" (Micah 6:4 NIV).

4. *Miriam had a very special position among her people. What was it?*

Miriam had a position of leadership and was one of the first women ministry leaders. She led the people in worship as they crossed the Red Sea, which included leading the women who joined in with their timbrels and in the dance. There may also have been other times not recorded that she also led the people in worship to God. She was the people's worship leader.

5. *Miriam demonstrated a very powerful method of worship after crossing the Red Sea. Why do you think she chose dance as her method of showing appreciation?*

When you are excited, it is very hard to stay in one place for too long. To witness the rolling back of the sea on the army must have been unbelievable and overwhelming for the people, resulting in them jumping and dancing around in an uncontrollable manner. Miriam, who also witnessed it with excitement, took control of the situation and turned it into a wonderful time of dance and praise to God.

For the women, this would have been a demonstration of their faith and new freedom. They had been slaves for so many years and when you are a slave, you do as you are told, not what you want to do or feel that you should do. These women had just received an incredible gift from their God, for they were finally safe and, above all, free! They were giving thanks to God with their entire beings, so this would not have been just a dance but also part of the prayer. It is also remarkable that this battle would have been won with absolutely no human loss of life of their people. This battle was the Lord's and he had won it completely.

When we watch cultural dancing—no matter if it is in Canada, Hawaii, Asia or the Middle East—the one thing in common is that the dance tells a story. As these women gave praise through the dance, they, like the cultures just mentioned, would likely have been telling the story of what had just happened as well. It was very common to celebrate the victory of battle with dance and song.

6. ***What is the significance of the instrument—the timbrels—that Miriam used to lead her dance?***

Like a tambourine, a timbrel was a percussion instrument that had bells, rings, or metal discs attached to make a ringing noise when shaken or tapped by the hand. It also had ribbons, tassels or streamers attached for decoration. The women, especially the young and unmarried girls, primarily used this instrument. The Bible refers to it being used in dance as well as in praise and worship. Psalm 150 refers to the tambourine being used for praise in his sanctuary. Timbrels were also often used to celebrate military success. Therefore, it would have been logical to bring out timbrels and celebrate the victory over the army and the beginning of their new freedom.

7. ***In what ways do we demonstrate worship to God today?***

Worship means many things to people today. For some of us, our methods of worship are not so different from the methods that Miriam used. Many use instruments, voices, clapping of hands and dancing. Some prefer to stand up, raise their hands and be very demonstrative, while others may want to sit quietly and sing softly. There is no right or wrong method because God doesn't care about our methods but about the fact that we do it.

8. ***How did Miriam react under Moses' leadership?***

In the beginning, Miriam was very happy to be serving God under Moses. Yet, as time went on, that spirit of envy and greed tried to worm its way into her heart and mind and she eventually began to listen to it. This is when she started to question why Moses was in charge. However, the fact remained that God put Moses in charge, not Miriam, and she needed to respect the one whom God appointed. As she got more and more upset with Moses, she wanted to try to take over some of the leadership. What is strange about this action is that Miriam must have known that, as a woman in that time period, the men would never permit her to be the leader.

9. *What did Moses do that made Miriam and Aaron angry enough to want to mutiny?*

The problems climaxed when Moses went up the mountain to receive the Ten Commandments from God and the people felt that he was taking too long to come back down. The longer he was gone, the greater the dissention grew, resulting in Aaron gathering all of the gold in camp to make a golden calf for worship. Aaron knew that it was wrong, yet he blamed the people when Moses came back and questioned him. Prior to that, Miriam and Aaron were very unhappy with the fact that Moses had married a Cushite woman who had darker skin than they did. In my opinion, these two were looking for something wrong, and if it hadn't been Moses' wife, it would have been something else. These two had a huge case of envy that revealed itself when they asked if God spoke to Moses more than he spoke to them. When Miriam and Aaron started to second-guess God's decisions, it became their biggest mistake.

10. *What were the consequences of her actions?*

For one week, Miriam suffered with leprosy, totally isolating her family and friends. People would see her as almost less than human and definitely dirty. She had to leave her home and live in a leper colony, which was located well away from her family and friends. If anyone other than lepers came near her, she would have to yell "unclean!" to warn them to stay back.

11. *Why do think that only Miriam experienced punishment when Aaron was guilty too?*

Miriam's punishment was not only because of the fact that she criticized her brother's interracial marriage, but also because of her haughtiness and her refusal to recognize the chain of command that God had established. Miriam and Aaron became extremely irritated with Moses' great calling and position, asking, "Has the Lord indeed spoken only by Moses? Has he not spoken also by us? And the Lord heard it" (Numbers 12:2.NKJV).As you read these words, you can almost hear the sarcasm in their voices. In verse 1, it says Miriam first then Aaron—not the other way around as you might expect since men were held in higher regard than women were. Because it reads in this order, perhaps we are to understand that Miriam initiated the criticism.

As you read on, you find out that Aaron was the first to notice the leprosy on Miriam. At that moment, he must have become afraid for himself as well, because just as quickly as he acknowledged Miriam's situation, he asked for mercy for both of them, not just for her. Numbers 12:11-12 says, "So Aaron said to Moses, 'Oh, my lord! Please do not lay this sin on us, in which we have done foolishly and in which we have sinned. Please do not let her be as one dead, whose flesh is half consumed when he comes out of his mother's womb!'" Had he not repented so quickly, maybe he, too, would have experienced God's punishment—but that we can only guess.

12. *Do you think that Miriam's punishment had an effect on Aaron? If so, what?*

The term "scared straight" is probably appropriate here. Even though he felt some form of consequence, he must have known that it could have been worse. Knowing that his sister had been stricken with leprosy must have scared him, since it could also have been him.

13. *What do the following scriptures teach us about criticizing others and overestimating our own importance?*

Proverbs 30:12—We are saved but we are not perfect; we are all still sinners in need of God's grace. We need to take a good look at ourselves because no matter how good we think we are there is still evil within us. Luke 6:41-42 also warns us about criticizing someone for their wrongdoings when we are doing just as bad or worse.

Luke 18:11—Be careful not to judge one another, for none of us is free of failure. Luke 6:41 asks us "Why do you look at the speck of sawdust in your brother's eye and pay no attention to the plank in your own eye?" The Pharisee thought that the tax collector was so evil and that he was so perfect and we see that throughout his entire prayer, he actually thanked God for not making him like the tax collector. What he really needed to do was to not worry about the tax collector, but rather, about what he was doing and the attitude with which he was doing it.

Romans 12:3—We are no better than anyone else around us. We have all sinned and come short of the glory of God but he still wants to shower us with his blessings and ever-loving kindness.

Philippians 2:3-4—We need to be humble, not brag about what we have done or how we have done it.

These four scriptures all say that we need to watch what we say about others and how we think about ourselves. We need to watch how we treat others and realize that we are all sinners—none of us is any better than the other. Even the worst sinner, when he or she comes to God and asks forgiveness, is pure in his eyes. When we try to let everyone know how bad another person is (in other words—gossiping), we make ourselves look bad instead. So be careful whom you are criticizing.

17. *What do you think the following scriptures are trying to tell us?*

Romans 12:1—God shows us mercy each day and, in turn, we are to be obedient to his word. We must keep ourselves a living sacrifice to him and not become man-focused. Our lives are to honour God and to allow him to use us in the way that he wants.

1 Corinthians 12—Before we become believers, we do our own thing, not thinking about anyone but ourselves because we think that there is no one else to answer to. As we come to Christ, we find out that we are not alone; God is there and he has special gifts, ministries and activities (v. 4-6) ready for each of us. He has given us these gifts through the working of the Holy Spirit in our lives. Jeremiah 1:4 says that God knew us before we were in our mother's womb and then, in Jeremiah 29:11, God says he has plans for us. When someone has a plan for you, he or she gives you the tools to carry out the plan or, at the very least, tells you how to get them for yourself. God is no different and our gifts may be manifested in different ways according to the work that he has for us to further his kingdom. The Spirit decides which gifts are given to each person, but people have been given free choice and can decide for themselves whether they will honour the Spirit and use their gifts. We need to acknowledge these gifts and realize from whom they came, then use them to the best of our abilities.

Ephesians 4—We are to live the life to which we have been called. We need to live our lives in humility, being gentle, peaceful and accepting of others. When we first believed, we were like newborn babies; now we need to continually grow and mature into adults. This is as we age, not only in human years, but also in spiritual years. When each of us grows and does the work that we are to do using our God-given talents, the entire body of Christ grows and matures. We leave behind the way that we were before Christ and become new with him as our leader.

4

An Unexpected Messenger

Chapter Objective

Jesus is there for us and doesn't care where we have been or what we have done in the past. The important thing is what we are going to do in the future as we turn our lives over to him.

Future Study Focus

Salvation belongs to God and is a gift from him to us. If you want it, it is available, but you must want it honestly and not be a hypocrite about it.

Questions

1. *We are never told the name of the Woman at the Well. Why do you think that is?*

Her actual name is of no significance to the story. We are told that she was a Samaritan who was avoided by most people. We know that she was ostracized by the townspeople for her many husbands and her living conditions. We know that she didn't have a great deal of money because people of wealth would not have gone to get their own water but would have had their servants go for them. We know that Jesus had a message about living water just for her. We know that Jesus used her to bring others in the town to the true God. Would we have focused on all of this if we had known her name, or would we have had to know the meaning of her name, the family from which she came and so on? God does not want us to focus on the name of the person but rather on the fact that, like us, she wasn't perfect, yet he had a plan and purpose for her life.

2. Even though we may not be able to call her by name, how well do you think the Lord knew her? (Also read Psalm 139-13-16 and Jeremiah 1:5.)

God knows everything about us even before we come to him; so, of course, he already knew everything about this woman. Jesus revealed this when he told her to go and get her husband and she told him that she had no husband. He responded with the comment that he knew that and that her answer was right and honest. Jesus told her all about her life as they conversed, so he knew everything that there was to know. Since God knows everything and Jesus is God, then he knew it all before they even met. Even so, he still spoke to her with compassion, letting her tell her story.

7. Scripture tells us that this woman left her water jug behind when she went to tell the townspeople what had just happened. What do you think is the significance of her leaving it rather than carrying it with her?

As she spoke with Jesus, she had her eyes opened to the true God and she had to share the new information with the people in her town. Leaving the water jug behind as she ran to tell them signified that she was leaving her past at the well. When she left the well, she was a new person, one who was now clean. When we accept Jesus into our hearts, our sins are forgiven; that was the case for this woman—she left her sins at the well.

8. Knowing the way the townspeople had treated this woman, why do you think she even bothered to tell them about Jesus, let alone rushing to tell them?

Just like many people today, when this woman accepted Jesus, she wanted to tell everyone about her new love. She didn't just get a new set of clothes to renew the outside but salvation brought her a renewal from the inside out. In the midst of experiencing these new emotions, this woman didn't care what had taken place in the past. She felt different and she had to get her news out and tell someone, anyone—even those who had hurt her before!

5

A Wise Peacemaker

Chapter Objective

We must always be on guard and ready to move for God. We must not just jump into situations but use our wisdom and thought before we react. When we do, God will honour and bless us.

Future Study Focus

The use of wisdom must become a part of our everyday lives. Wisdom carries a great deal of power when used correctly and brings blessings to the one who uses it well.

Questions

2. *A person's words can teach us a lot about him or her. What do you think the words of Nabal, David and Abigail say about them? What do your words to others say about you?*

Nabal's words confirm that he really was a fool. David was protecting Nabal's land and livestock; yet Nabal thought he could disregard David and say no when he asked him for food for his men. Being drunk may have affected how much his mouth runneth over but not completely.

When Nabal refused him, David's words revealed the magnitude of his temper. In his anger, he was going to have his men kill not only

187

Nabal but all of the men with him as well. David displayed a soft spot for Abigail since he listened when she went to him and later called for her to be his wife.

Abigail was a peacemaker. She was wise and showed good judgment when she took it upon herself to go to David to try to correct what her husband had done. She knew the exact words to use to be very convincing. She used her wisdom and her ability to articulate to get David's attention and keep him from committing a crime that would compromise his royal makeup. She had finally had enough of Nabal and his constant demonstration of his foolishness.

3. *Abigail and Nabal seem completely incompatible as a couple. How do women today respond when they find themselves married to men like Nabal? If different from your answer above, how do you think they should handle it?*

(Leaders, you may have to limit the amount of time you allow for discussion on this question, as it could open up quite a hornet's nest.)

Suggested answer:

Many women who find themselves married to someone who is very different from themselves end up separating from their husbands. However, there are also those who are actually attracted to their opposite and instead of it being a problem, it turns out favourably.

When you are with a man like Nabal, who is a fool—outspoken when it is better to be quiet—you then have two options. You can work with it, like Abigail did, doing your best to smooth things out when he speaks when he should have kept quiet. However, this can be a problem if you find that you are always on edge waiting for the next ball to drop. The other solution is to be open and honest with your husband about his actions since he might not realize what he is doing. Together, you can come up with a method to work with him to help him. When you do this, you are accepting that you are in this marriage for the long haul.

4. *From everything that we have read about the relationship between David and Nabal, do you think David's request to Nabal for provisions for himself and his men was realistic?*

The story tells us that David did not initially intend to harm Nabal or anyone associated with him. David had been protecting Nabal's livelihood and the men who worked for him and there was no indication that this relationship would end soon. When David sent his men to Nabal, he addressed Nabal as "my brother," which was a gesture of peace toward Nabal, his household and all of his belongings. What David was asking for was like payment for all that he had done for Nabal. He wasn't asking for the moon but was being very reasonable.

5. *David snapped a response to Nabal, which was reactionary rather than necessarily correct. (1 Samuel 25:12-13) What does Luke 6:27-31 say that we are to do when someone treats us unfairly?*

We are to pray for our enemies and do good to those who don't like us. When someone treats us badly or curses us, we are to bless him or her. If someone takes something of ours, then we are not to ask for it back but to ask God to bless him or her. When we don't let the hurt go, it only grows and turns into bitterness. The Word says that if someone slaps one cheek we are to offer him or her the other. This means that if someone hurts us, we are not to give up on him or her. Is there anything too hard for our God to do? If that relationship is to be restored through our love for that person, it will happen. We need to realize that sometimes God needs us to let someone go so that we can move on to do greater things for him with someone else.

7. *Thinking back to my grandmother's favorite phrase, "The easiest words to take back in the morning are those that are left unsaid," are there are times when this statement does not apply?*

The only time watching your words can be a mistake is if someone is heading toward something detrimental to his or her health or well-being. In this case, to say nothing because you don't want to get involved or hurt his or her feelings is very wrong. In reference to one's children, Barbara Coloroso suggests "if it is not illegal, immoral or life threatening, there is no need to worry." If we take these three terms as a guide, we will be much better off.

8. *When Abigail went to David, she demonstrated great resourcefulness but also faced great danger. What risks do you think she took in approaching David and his men?*

David was so angry with Nabal that the very sight of Abigail could have brought his wrath down on her. She took the risk of David calling for her immediate death. She added to the risk when she asked David to take his anger and place it onto her. She took the blame for not having the food ready for David's men when they came. The risks didn't end with David either, because Nabal was a man with a violent temper and she was part of his household. After Nabal found out what she did, she may have felt his rage since he was drunk at the time and women were never to contradict their husband's wishes.

9. *She knew the words to use to get under David's skin. What were those statements and why do you think that they influenced David so much?*

To begin with, Abigail acknowledged David and asked him to shift the blame from Nabal to her. She continued and said that she would have prepared the food for David and his men earlier if she had only seen them. This let David know that not everyone regarded him as poorly as Nabal did. She told David that she thought that Nabal was a fool and that even his name meant fool. The fact that Abigail was willing to have the blame shifted to her from Nabal, even though he was a fool, demonstrated courage to David and helped him to see things in a different light. She also reminded him that vengeance should be from God and not from man. He took that to heart and as he saw the food and heard her words, his heart changed from bitterness and wanting instant revenge to respect for Abigail and recognizing Nabal as a joke and the fool he really was.

11. *There is a fine line between meddling and helping. At what point do you think it is good to step in and speak out on behalf of others?*

Sometimes people don't want our help or advice. I think the time is right when the result of the disagreement is going to have long-term or permanent repercussions. If this disagreement is ending a friendship or splitting family members, then it is important for someone to come in and break the ice. When the situation arises, go to the person and ask if you can make a suggestion, but be sure to first ask God for wisdom and guidance. Again, if it involves something immoral, illegal or life-threatening then you can carefully—using wisdom—tread in.

12. *Who did Abigail help by her actions?*

Abigail saved her husband because it was not David who caused his demise but rather God who dealt with him for being such a fool. She also saved all of the men who were with Nabal because David had called for all of their deaths. Finally, she saved herself and all of the other women and families in the community since, once a husband was lost, unless there was a son to take care of her, the woman and her children found it very hard to live and were often destitute.

6

Obedient & Trusting—Twice Over

Chapter Objective

We may not always know the reasons why, but we know that we must trust in God.

Future Study Focus

2 Samuel 22:31—God and his ways are perfect and his word has been repeatedly proven. Even sceptical scientists can't deny the Word since science has proven many biblical facts and stories. God has given us his Word to be a guide and a sword, and scripture tells us that he is the Word. John 1:1 (NKJV) says: "In the beginning was the Word, and the Word was with God, and the Word was God." If we really believe that, then we will rely on the Word to be our guide because God cannot tell any lies.

Questions

1. *Why do you think God had Elijah ask this widow for bread even though he knew how very desperate she was?*

   In Luke 16, the Word says that if we can be trusted with little things then we will be trusted with greater things. This woman's actions proved her trust in God. Before she could have the promise of a never-ending container of oil and flour, she had to take the step of faith, make bread with the little she had left and then give it away.

For her to be able to be that faithful, she had to feel God's hand on her life. How much did she really trust God to supply her needs? The answer is obviously "a lot!" since she did give Elijah the bread that he asked for. God told Elijah that he had "commanded" her to provide him with food (NIV). She had no idea what was coming, since she thought that she was gathering firewood to make her last meal, but God had set up this appointment with a prophet so that he could bless her. God wanted to bless her with a miracle and to perform it he wanted to bring it to her from nothing.

2. *This woman knew very well that she might be preparing her last meal, so why did she say yes to this man's request for food?*

Sometimes you can feel in the pit of your stomach that you should do something. You may not understand why because it may be something that is out of character for you. Perhaps that is what happened to this woman. She knew that it was her last meal and then she was expecting to die anyway, so if this meal could help a man of God continue, then she knew that she had to do it. She may have thought that it would not make any difference to her or her son and her unexplainable feelings were too strong to ignore. The Spirit of God was influencing her, creating a desire to be faithful to him.

To be completely faithful, we must serve him with whatever we have, no matter how small it may seem. As God saw her heart, he knows our hearts, sees our efforts and knows the attitudes from which we operate. If God is leading you to do something, do it for his glory even if it feels small or insignificant to you. He wants to bless you and reward you for your faithfulness. Who knows—God may be preparing you for something bigger than you could ever imagine!

5. *In addition to the grief of losing her son, what emotions do you think this woman experienced after her son died? Do you think she felt abandoned and let down? Do you think she felt lost and alone?*

A feeling of complete abandonment may have been this woman's greatest emotion. She must have wondered how she would ever survive. What would she do? Where would she live? How would she ever find food to eat? When she lost her husband, her son was to take care of her, but now he was gone too. Now destitute, she must have felt great fear and uncertainty about her future. Deep down, she knew that God had already saved her during the drought and famine, but would he be there for her this time? We can only guess that she tried to keep up her faith, but sometimes fear overpowers even those with great faith.

6. *She was looking to place blame on someone for her new situation. On whom did she place it—on God, Elijah or perhaps her sins?*

In 1 Kings 17:18, the widow says, "What have I to do with you, O man of God? Have you come to me to bring my sin to remembrance, and to kill my son?"(NKJV). I believe that in her grief, she blamed her sins but also blamed Elijah since she said, "What have I to do with you?" It sounds like she believed that if she hadn't had anything to do with him in the first place, then maybe none of this would have happened and any sin that she had would have been kept hidden and silent.

8. *Do you see ways that you can practise your faith today even if you do not feel stretched?*

There are times each day that we can and must rely on our faith. Every time we go into an important meeting at work, write an exam at school or even walk into our homes after being away, we have faith that we will succeed or be safe. Faith is something that must be a part of our everyday routine.

9. *Do you believe that stretching is how we grow in Christ and that without it we can stagnate and start to take things for granted?*

If everything stayed the same day in and day out, it would not only become very boring—there is no way that we would ever change. Why would we when we know what to expect and when to expect it? When things come into our lives that surprise us, then we have an opportunity to be challenged, increase our knowledge and purify our talents. Challenges allow our talents and gifts to develop to the next level and/or multiply as we discover new ones.

10. *When tested a second time, as happened to this woman, do you think people have a tendency to forget the miracles of the past? Why do you think their faith wavers?*

The first reaction when tested a second time is often "This can't be happening again! I can't do this again!" The miracles that initially happened can be forgotten when the overwhelming panic that sets in is allowed to overtake the situation.

11. *For the second time, this woman saw God move radically on her behalf. What was the reaction of the widow when her son was returned to her? What do you think happened to her faith?*

Initially, she must have been so excited at having her son restored that through her tears of joy she would be crying out her thanks and praise to God. At that moment, her faith would have been immense and she would have told everyone that her God had taken care of her. However, it is possible that this confidence did not last. We as humans have very short memories, and though she would always remember that her son had been raised from the dead, the fact that God did it may have become secondary to her still having her son. Too often, our faith is only as good as the next crisis and then, unfortunately, the process must begin all over again.

12. *The second widow gave two coins in the offering. Why were those coins so significant?*

Jesus was sitting opposite the offering box and saw not only what she was depositing but also what the scribes were putting in. They were giving the obligatory ten percent; this woman, on the other hand, was giving it all. This was her whole life; she gave out of her poverty since there was no such thing as a rich widow. Women owning nothing were reliant on their sons or other male relatives to care for them. The Greek word for widow, chera, is from the root ghe, which means "forsaken" or "left empty." Once she gave these coins, she had absolutely nothing.

These two coins demonstrate the importance of the attitude in which you give. For the scribes, giving their ten percent meant nothing to them other than to reinforce their self-righteousness. However, when the widow gave her last two coins, she showed trust—either she would die now or God would take care of her.

When Jesus tells this story to his disciples, I don't think he is necessarily affirming poverty, but rather, he is telling them that these people have become unnoticeable to society and that this is wrong. He used her as an example of love for God, and the scribes needed to take note because they would be judged on how they treated this woman as well as other widows, orphans and even strangers. It's possible that Jesus also saw her action as a picture of what he was going to do for all of us. Just as she gave everything she had for the offering, Jesus gave up everything he had in heaven to come to earth and then to die for you and me.

13. *Why was Jesus even watching what people were putting into the offering?*

There was a lesson that needed to be taught and this event gave him an opportunity to illustrate it. In Matthew 23:14, Jesus described the pompous scribes as those who devour widows' houses and then make long prayers just to look good, which was probably why they gave too—just to look good. Their giving wasn't from the heart as was this woman's. She was quiet and meek while the scribes were ceremoniously pretentious, which intrigued Jesus to watch even more.

15. *What does the Word say about giving from the heart?*

Matthew 6:3-4 (NKJV) says that when we give, we need to give as if we are doing it in secret. It doesn't mean that we can't give in church because someone might see what we are doing, but it does mean that we need to check our attitude when we give. Are you giving so others will see and think you are wonderful because of what you are doing? Alternatively, are you really giving to the Lord?

If you have ever decided to give a set amount into an offering and then all of a sudden felt very strongly that you should give more—that was the Holy Spirit speaking to you. When you listen to him, you are giving from the heart, trusting that it will be okay. You also don't really care who sees it because once it leaves your hands it is no longer yours but God's. He will direct the receiver of the cash on how to distribute it and if the church or organization doesn't use it properly then they have to answer to God not to us. When God calls someone to ministry, the Word says that he or she will be judged greater than the average person will. Therefore, when we give to the church, as the pastor and councils decide where to spend it, they have to follow their conscience and the leading of the Holy Spirit just as you did in giving it.

16. *Why did Jesus see a greater value in this woman's gift compared to some of the larger ones?*

When the poor women gave her last two coins, she made a true sacrifice since it really was all she had. When the rich man gave it probably didn't even put a dent in his pocketbook, so it definitely didn't hurt him to give. He would have gone home, had his dinner and forgot about his gift. I think the other reason is, once again, the attitude of giving. When she gave, she gave with a total attitude of submission to God; yet when he gave, it may have been because he wanted others to notice that he was giving or just because he felt that his action reflected something good. In Jesus' eyes, the attitude of the giver added or took away from the value of the gift.

17. *What guidelines concerning giving appear in the following scriptures?*

Exodus 25:2: The people were to bring gifts of their choosing to God.

1 Chronicles 29:14: Everything we have really comes from God; so when we give, we are just giving back to him what is really his anyway.

Matthew 6:2-4: Give because you want to, not because someone will see you. When you give for the sake of others seeing you, their recognition will be your only reward. God sees your gift and he sees your attitude, so give in secret, or at least make sure you do not flash your gift around. God will see your gift and that is all that matters.

1 Corinthians 16:2: Save for the future to be ready when God calls on you. Plan every week what you are going to give and make sure that you have it put away so that you don't have to panic looking for it later.

2 Corinthians 9:6-7: Give joyfully from your heart. You will reap what you have sown from your giving.

We need to invest what we can in God's kingdom. If we have much, we should give much; if we have little, we should give what we can. It isn't so much the amount we have to give but rather the attitude in which we give what we have that counts.

Determination

Chapter Objective

A complete demonstration of perseverance and determination while waiting for an answer to prayer.

Future Study Focus

When they are ill, God can heal our children and keep them safe in their day-to-day activities. We need to give them to him in prayer and then let him work on them. He wants to bless them no matter how old they are. Even at 50, you are somebody's child.

Questions

1. *How did this woman represent her crisis to Jesus? Do you think she outlined the urgency of it well?*

This woman saw Jesus passing by and repeatedly called out to him. She told him that her daughter was demon-possessed and needed his help right now. She cried out, telling him that she was really suffering, which does indicate the urgency of the problem. She could have expressed herself much differently without actually accosting him as he and the disciples went by, but she was desperate as she had tried everything else and still the demons held on. They say that desperate times call for desperate measures and that is exactly what this woman did. She could not and would not give up on her daughter because she wanted her back and she knew that this was the man who could do it.

2. *Why do you think she called Jesus "Lord, the Son of David"?*

When she called him this, she was actually acknowledging who he really was—Jesus, the Messiah, King of the Jews. She had obviously heard about him. She may have thought that if she acknowledged that she knew who he was, that he would stop, listen and then help her.

4. *List the barriers that she had to overcome before getting the action that she needed.*

Culture was the first barrier—this woman was not a Jew, but a Canaanite. The Old Testament tells us that the Canaanites had been longtime enemies of Israel. In the back of her mind, she must have wondered if he would help her since Jesus was for the Jews. Second, when she did call out to Jesus with her petition, he completely ignored her. He didn't tell her to go away; he just ignored her, leaving her to think that maybe he wouldn't help her. Next, the disciples were tired, irritable and wanted time to themselves without anyone asking for anything. They asked Jesus to send her away so that they could have some peace and quiet. Fourth, when she finally got Jesus to speak to her, he emphatically told her that he was not there for her people, so why should he take the time to heal her child? Finally, she had to stand her ground through the rest of the conversation—almost argumentatively—to convince him that her child needed help and that he was the one who could do it.

5. *How did she get over each of the hurdles?*

This woman didn't run from any of the obvious hurdles. She acknowledged them, but she refused to give up. She addressed each of Jesus' comments head-on and came back with her answer. She acknowledged who Jesus was and that he had come for the Jews, but that didn't stop her from pleading for an exception and a pouring out of his mercy to her daughter. She continued to state her need and seemed to have an answer for everything that Jesus threw at her.

7. *How did Jesus pay tribute to her?*

In the end, Jesus did two things for this woman. He first healed her daughter, which is what she was pleading for. However, he also told her that she was a woman of GREAT faith, which was a real honour for her, especially since she was a Canaanite—a Gentile, not a Jew.

8. *What does this story tell us about faith?*

We do need to pray about situations and make sure that we are in God's will, but then we are to persevere and not give up. If I ask someone for something once and then give up, the person may feel that it was just a whim; but if I am constantly asking, it is evident that this request is important to me. I wonder if God isn't the same way.

11. *How can we show the same kind of persistent faith that this woman had so that we also receive our answer?*

It is so important that we nurture an ongoing relationship with God and keep communication open through prayer and spending time in his Word. That means constantly speaking with him through prayer and praise. We also need to get into his Word, whether by listening to audio recordings, reading or studying different versions. The method of study isn't as important as just doing it!

12. *This is not just a story of wonderful healing; it is also a story of the love and tenacity of a mother who never gave up. As parents, we need to not give up on our kids and to always lift them up to God. What do the following verses tell us about children and prayer?*

The Scripture examples include individuals praying or who have prayed for their children. Some wanted Jesus to bless them; others wanted to have a child. I think this tells us that no matter how old or where our kids are, there is a constant and continual need to lift them up to God in prayer. We are never too old for a parent's prayer. God wants to hear us pray and our kids need to know that we remember them.

8

Leadership and Hospitality

Chapter Objective

In *Matthew 28:19*, Jesus told his disciples to *"Go therefore and make disciples of all the nations, baptizing them in the name of the Father and of the Son and of the Holy Spirit."* When we become Christians, that command is also for us to do our part in whatever way we can. Lydia did just that, giving her home, her time, her resources, her staff and her entire being to the advancement of the Kingdom of God.

Future Study Focus

Leadership, Leadership, Leadership. We all have the capability to lead something or someone. Look for those abilities and use them the best way possible. While leading, keep focused on God. He will be there helping you because no one can do it alone. Remember, don't lead with a haughty attitude and don't get discouraged—lead with a little lean toward God in your step.

Questions

1. *What was Lydia's hometown? (One of the seven churches of Asia was located there.)*

Lydia lived in the city of Thyatira, which was known for its markets.

2. *What was noteworthy about Lydia's profession?*

Lydia was a seller of very valuable purple fabric. She was an employer, not an employee. The fabric that she sold was only available to the very rich since they were the only ones who could afford such cloth. Everyone has their favourite store to shop in, maybe because of the people or the products. That is how the wealthy felt about Lydia.

4. *From Paul's reaction to this group, what can we determine were his views on women?*

Many Pharisees felt that men should not speak to women in public unless they were related. Other men of that day felt that women were to be treated as possessions to be used for their needs, not to be respected or listened to. Paul could have been one of these men but I don't think he was. Being a teacher, he spent time in the synagogues on the Sabbath day telling people about Jesus; yet on this particular Sabbath, he couldn't attend because there wasn't one around. He could have given up and left town but he didn't do that; instead, he went out to the river and found not men but women who believed in God gathered for prayer. If he had been a typical man of the time, he would not have stayed with these women, but stay he did, and he shared the Word with them. He treated them as close to counterparts as they could be treated in that day. It was Paul who wrote to the Galatians, *"There is neither Jew nor Greek, there is neither slave, nor free, there is neither male nor female; for you are all one in Christ Jesus" (Gal 3:28).* In these words, we can see and hear that Paul is really pushing for equality amongst people of all kinds, including women.

7. *What is the significance of the fact that Lydia was not only the first convert in Europe, but was also female?*

In that culture, women were not thought of as leaders except in their households. To give Lydia that notoriety of being the first convert is in extreme contradiction to that society, yet, it is what we might expect from God. We see in other passages how he uses the poor, the injured—even children—so we can imagine that he would use a woman. He demonstrated the significance of how important women were to the church then and still are today.

8. ***As soon as she became a believer, she immediately did two things (v. 15). What were they?***

Lydia immediately brought her family and servants so that they could be baptized. She then invited Paul and his friends to stay with her and, as we say today, she wouldn't take "no" for an answer.

9. ***Lydia showed great hospitality to Paul and his friends. What difference did this make to them?***

Before we can understand the real significance of what she did, we must first understand what hospitality really is. Hospitality is the gift of being able to welcome and courteously serve friends and strangers alike. The Greek word for "hospitable" means "lover of strangers," "friend of strangers," or "fond of guests." The English word "hospitality" has the same root word—"hospice" and "hospital"— which makes me think of caregiving and healing. Hospitable people are those who take pleasure in entertaining strangers as well as family and friends. The hospitable person doesn't get upset with the guests who just drop in, but finds enjoyment in providing food as well as lodging for their physical comforts.

Even outside the home, hospitable people can be seen making someone they don't know or have just met feel welcome. You can pick them out on Sunday mornings because they are the ones who always go up to the strangers to say hi and welcome them into your church. In extending food, shelter, rest and good conversation, one is providing a place for people to be healed from the pains and sorrows of this life.

Paul and his followers now had a place to stay for as long as they liked so that they could focus on the work that they were meant to be doing, which was sharing the news of Jesus. Even after they were in jail, they knew that there was a place waiting for them and that their work could continue. Lydia became the hotel, the church and the restaurant. They had nothing to worry about for as long as they chose to stay.

10. *Why was she so anxious for them to stay with her?*

Because Lydia had the gift of hospitality, she wanted to make sure others received everything that they needed. The only way that her family and the other people with whom she worshipped could receive the best was for Paul to stay and share the Word with them. She knew that she had heard it and accepted it, but she did not know enough to teach as effectively as Paul could. I believe that she had a true missionary's heart, wanting to see the Word shared with as many as could hear and then receive. She would do anything to make that happen. She told them that if they found her faithful, they would stay with her. She had proved her faithfulness with the desire to listen, learn and then immediately be baptized.

11. *Her new ministry was influential to two groups of people. Who were they?*

The first was the group of people around her—her staff and family members and the second was Paul and his entourage. She made provision for the first group to be fed by having the Word shared by a man of God, and then for Paul and those with him she provided the blessing of her hospitality.

12. *John 15:1-16 talks about the fruit and the vine. How did Lydia's life and works create fruit in those around her?*

In *The Message*, this verse reads, "I am the Vine, you are the branches. When you're joined with me and I with you, the relation intimate and organic, the harvest is sure to be abundant." Jesus is saying that when we join with him, we will be able to do much for the kingdom. And that is just what Lydia did. As soon as she became a believer, she started her work for the Lord. She shared her faith with her family and her servants. She opened her home to whoever needed it and listened to the message from these men of God. She opened her doors once again when Paul and Silas came out of prison. She continued to be of service to the church and the church people however she was needed and for as long as she was able. Lydia had a true servant's heart.

When you look at a fruit tree, the first thing you see is a very sturdy trunk with its roots going deep into the ground so that it can stand tall and firm as the branches extend from the body. Jesus is like that trunk; he is the vine who is strong and able to hold onto us as we branch off in new directions. Lydia's new life was like a one of those new branches, ready to blossom and produce new fruit any way she could. As she invested in the lives of the people and the disciples, she helped another blossom to produce a tasty piece of fruit. We never know how we will be used to help others to grow and we need to not get discouraged, but rather, remember: one plants, another waters, but God gives the increase, as he did with Lydia.

13. *Usually the words from Luke 12:48 are considered to be directed toward those in a pastoral ministry. Do you think that is the only interpretation for them? If not, then explain.*

This verse may only be meant for pastors, but since we are all called to minister, we all need to take heed. To each of us, a gift has been given and we need to use it to the best of our ability. God judges people on their own ability, not that of others.

14. *How does the story of Lydia affect women becoming involved in ministry today?*

Lydia's life message is twofold for women in ministry. First, it should be an encouragement that God can and will use anyone if we are only ready and willing. Second, it goes to show that we need to be ready at all times for the calling of God. We need to use what we have to help the ministry in any way that we can. It doesn't mean that we have to give large sums of money or take off and go thousands of miles away (unless you are called to do that, of course). Lydia stayed home and did the same job she was doing before she turned to Jesus and, in doing so, she was a very powerful witness. We can do the same—in the same job, attending the same church and with the same circle of friends. We can be a mighty witness for God by just being ready and willing to do as he directs. My pastor once said, "If you don't like women in leadership you are in the wrong place." Like him, many pastors today are realizing the importance of the work that the women do in the church and are encouraging women to step up and do the work that God has called them to do.

Loyalty

Chapter Objective

Jesus helped to break down the gender barriers of his time. He allowed women to play an important role in the early church and, consequently, the church today.

Future Study Focus

Make the Word of Jesus known, but watch your step so that you don't fill your heart with envy, arrogance or other temptations. Jesus said that he will never leave us alone, so we can move on, praising and rejoicing in his name. As we do good for God, we, in turn, will be blessed.

Questions

2. *Joanna and the others demonstrated their appreciation for their healing. What can we do? What should we do?*

Joanna responded to her healing by completely giving herself to the ministry of Jesus, supporting and following him wherever he went. She was ready and willing to do whatever he asked whenever he asked. We should be ready for the call that God will place on our lives whenever and wherever he chooses. He may ask us to be a quiet witness or to share with thousands.

3. ***What do you think Joanna's life was like after she started to associate with Jesus, both when she was with Jesus and when she was at home?***

When she was with Jesus, Joanna's life felt exhilarating and wonderful, but when she went home, she had to face the questions and snide comments of Herod and Chuza. This also happens to women today when their husbands resent them going to church. When they are at church and with other Christians, they feel good and are happy, but when they get home, their husbands make their lives miserable, almost like punishment for doing something they enjoy.

4. ***Why would she continue to support Jesus and his men when she must have had to go through so much at home?***

It was a question of the good far outweighing the bad. She saw and knew the good that Jesus was doing and she wanted to be a part of it. As Jesus healed her and shared the message of hope with her, she wanted to be with him to learn more and then to share the message with all she could. She felt that she needed to help this man who had helped her so much. We have all experienced being drawn toward something or someone, as was the case for Joanna. She knew what Chuza and Herod were like, but she just had to be with Jesus.

5. ***Why do you think the disciples did not want to believe what these women were trying to tell them about the empty grave?***

Even though Jesus trusted these women as they travelled with him, the disciples saw them as JUST women who were always there. They were second-class citizens who were there to serve, not to be respected or taken seriously. They must have felt that if the grave was ever going to be empty, surely Jesus would show it to them first and not the women. After all, they were the disciples, his main men. The thoughts of Jesus returning to life after the violent death they had witnessed seemed like sheer nonsense to them. It's also possible that they couldn't see past their grief. They had seen Jesus raise other people from the dead but now he was dead and the feelings of complete defeat overpowered them.

6. *How would you describe Joanna to a group of people that had never heard of her?*

Joanna was a very gentle but exuberant woman. She was a true servant dedicated to the cause of Christ and would do anything she could to assist with his ministry. If she were alive today, I think she would be a prayer warrior and a giver of both time and finances, not one who had to be front and centre but one who would be happy to be in the background helping out wherever needed.

7. *Looking at the following scriptures, describe how we are to move on and out for God.*

Psalm 138:3—We need to ensure that we begin with prayer and then God will give us the strength and tenacity to go on.

Proverbs 28:1—The lion is called the king of the jungle and everyone listens to him as he roars. If we are as bold as lions, the world will listen to us.

Acts 13:46—If we share the Word of God with someone and he or she rejects it, then we are to be unafraid to say that if he or she won't listen, we will go to others who will.

Ephesians 6:20—It doesn't matter what restrictions are on us; we can still speak if that is what God wants us to do.

Hebrews 13:16—Don't get so consumed in sharing the Word that you forget to be generous; but remember to give and give sacrificially.

The one key word here is "bold." Most of these verses refer to becoming bold in speech and action.

8. *How do you think we achieve this boldness?*

The only way to achieve boldness is to build a relationship with God. Psalm 138:3 says, "I cried out," and then, "You answered." God answers me when I cry out to him, and the result is boldness and strength in my innermost being, my soul.

9. **With the attitudes toward women being so negative in those times, why do you think Jesus helped and worked with so many women?**

Jesus worked with and healed the underdogs: the poor, the homeless and the children. His inclusion of women illustrated how he can use anyone, no matter who or what he or she is, as long as that person is willing. The women were not only willing but also very capable, and they helped greatly to increase the work of Jesus while on this earth.

10. **Do you think these women have an influence on women in ministry today?**

Definitely! These women provide a foundation for all women in ministry today. They demonstrated courage to move out of their comfort zones when God called. These women give today's women hope and encouragement to move upward and outward for Jesus. We can see the beautiful way that Christianity has elevated the role of women all over the world. Women were the ones who stayed behind with Jesus when he was on the cross. Women were the ones preparing the necessary oils to anoint the body of Jesus. Women were the first to discover the empty tomb and see the angel outside of it. Women were the first to see the resurrected Lord, and it was women who first preached the Gospel as they returned, declaring the good news of the resurrection.

13. **In what ways, other than through our finances, can we serve the cause of Christ?**

If we really love God as we say we do, then only our imaginations and our willingness to move out in his name can limit our service to him. If the Holy Spirit leads you, then he will enable you. Any time you share the fruit of the Spirit (including love, joy, peace, long-suffering and meekness—see Galatians 5), you are helping the cause of Jesus.

Many people prefer to act in private or in secret, such as faithfully committing to pray for the staff and pastors of the church. If, while praying, the Holy Spirit places someone else in your mind, then make sure that you include that person. We are told to love our enemies so don't forget to pray for them as well.

A Surprise Gift

Chapter Objective

You never know when, where or how God will show you a blessing.

Future Study Focus

Not even death can keep you in the grave if God wants you resurrected. He is there in all things and through all things.

Questions

1. *This woman was not asking Jesus for help; in fact, she did not know him, so why would he stop to help her out of the blue? After all, he was with an entirely different group of people at the time.*

As Jesus passed by, the grief that this woman was experiencing was obvious and his heart was moved with compassion.

He may also have wanted to illustrate how he had complete power over the grave. When Jesus raised Jarius' daughter from her deathbed, she had just passed away and, in fact, had not even been moved. When he raised Lazarus, he had not only been dead for a period but had been in the grave for four days and his body had started to decompose. This widow's son had been moved from his deathbed but not yet placed into the grave. This demonstrates that it doesn't matter how long you have been dead; if Jesus wants to raise you he can. This illustration is not just for physical death but also for spiritual death, and it exemplifies that it doesn't matter where we are because it only takes one touch from the hand of Jesus to be raised up.

2. ***The story tells us that Jesus had "great compassion" for this woman. What does that term mean?***

Compassion is true sympathy for the suffering and intense sadness of others who are hurting physically, mentally or emotionally. It often includes feelings of regret and pity and a deep desire to help or reach out with a kind and loving attitude, trying to alleviate some of the pain felt by the suffering person. If this is the description of compassion, then great compassion must be that definition intensified. Therefore, we can say that great compassion is an extreme sympathy filled with empathy for another's suffering and pain, along with an immense desire to help wherever you can.

3. ***Why do you think that Jesus was so willing to help this woman even without being asked, while previously he turned away the Canaanite woman who was so desperate?***

The principle of testing our faith and seeing just how much we really want something was a factor with the Canaanite woman. How badly did she want her daughter healed and to what degree would she try to get it done? On the other hand, the widow of Nain expected nothing. In fact, she wasn't even aware of Jesus' presence because she was just so full of grief. Some say that because Mary, his mother, was a widow, Jesus had a special spot of compassion in his heart for widows. We don't know that for sure, but we do know that he helped both women in this case.

4. ***What does knowing that Jesus healed her son even though she was not a woman of great faith tell you about God's love for people?***

Jesus loves people more than we can ever imagine. If he didn't then why would he have ever left heaven to come to earth just to be loved, then hated; emulated, then beaten and spit upon; or called friend and teacher, only to have them then call for his death? Through this demonstration of great sympathy and love, we also learn that Jesus wants to bless people and pour his love into them, especially when they least expect it.

Prostitute Redeemed

Chapter Objective

God loves us too much to leave us where we are if we are only willing to change with his help. In addition, he will honour our obedience with blessing and mercy.

Future Study Focus

God's faithfulness to us is everlasting and insurmountable. We need to look to him with joy, rejoicing and praise.

Questions

1. *The spies were nothing to Rahab, so what prompted her to hide them and lie to the soldiers for them?*

    Rahab was a risk taker and lying to the soldiers was definitely a huge risk. She had heard of the God of Israel and felt that he was going to give her city to them, so in the beginning it may have been for self-preservation. Yet, she had a feeling that this God was real and that she needed to follow him.

3. *Why do you think God would use someone like Rahab when someone from a higher or more respected position may have been available?*

Like some of the other women we have looked at, Rahab may not have been the most influential woman, but she was willing. God doesn't care who you are or what you have done—he will accept anyone who comes to him in faith. Salvation is the idea and work of God, not generated by man in any way. Rahab's life is a demonstration to women all over the world today that you can never be so low that God can't use you.

4. *You may know someone who feels like Rahab. What would you say to her to help her to believe that God really wants to forgive her?*

Every one of us is a sinner; yet, God does not condemn us, so we need not condemn ourselves. He is waiting with loving arms wide open and ready to scoop us up. All we need to do is come and ask for his help and forgiveness. He wants to shower us with mercy, love and joy.

5. *God tells us not to judge one another. How hard is it, then, to be around those with colourful pasts or whose present behaviour we disagree with?*

It can be difficult at times to not instinctively judge someone's lifestyle choices with which we don't agree. It is so important that we remember that it isn't the person with whom we don't agree, but rather, the activity with which he or she is involved. It is also not our place to judge him or her, for how can we see the stick in his or her eye when we have a log in ours?

6. *Looking at Rahab's story, what words can we use to describe her character?*

Listener—As men entered her establishment, she would listen to what they were saying and as she listened, she learned.

Clever—She may have heard what these men said about God but may have asked the right questions to learn more. Because of the way that women were thought of, she would have had to ask questions discreetly.

Caring—She cared enough about her entire family that when she asked for protection for herself, she also asked for it for them.

Reformed—Before Rahab's transformation, she lived a life of idolatry, but after, she was a changed person. She never returned to her old way of life, but rather, became a strong witness for God.

Strong-willed—We could describe her as headstrong since she would have had to be very courageous to speak to the soldiers the way she did. In fact, the name Rahab has been defined as "insolent," "fierce," "storm," "assault" and "arrogant."

9. ***Why do we still refer to her as "Rahab the prostitute" instead of by what she did or what she became?***

Rahab is a reminder that God can cleanse even the most contemptible sinner. He took someone who was living a life of immorality and made her an upright citizen. She is a witness to the fact that God is in the life-changing business.

10. ***After what Rahab did for them, why did the spies require an act of obedience from her? Why did they not immediately say that they would protect her house?***

The red cord may be thought of in the same way as the blood on the doorposts the night of the first Passover, when the firstborn male of every Egyptian died (Exodus 11-12). It was a symbol of just how far she was willing to go to save herself and her family. It may have also been a symbol of obedience for a new life.

11. ***How does Rahab's life demonstrate the statement that "God loves us too much to leave us where we are?"***

"By faith the harlot Rahab did not perish with those who did not believe, when she had received the spies with peace" (Hebrews 11:31 NKJV). God wants the best for us just as we want the best for our children.

Tears to Liberation

Chapter Objective

There is freedom in experiencing the forgiveness of our sins and excitement from knowing that, with this forgiveness, we are given a new life with God.

Future Study Focus

We may have lost ourselves in sin, but Jesus is there to bail us out when we call on him. He wants to see everyone saved, and when the lost come home, he rejoices and invites everyone else to rejoice along with him.

Questions

1. *Simon knew well the customs required each time a special guest entered his home. Why do you think he forgot or chose to ignore them when Jesus was his guest?*

When Jesus arrived, Simon held back any of the common courtesies that he would have dispensed to any of his other guests. It is very likely that he brought Jesus to the banquet with ulterior motives since the Pharisees really didn't like Jesus. Simon had reservations about the teaching of Jesus and wanted to see if he could trap him into some violation of the law. The Pharisees thought they were already wonderful people; consequently, they had no use for Jesus and his reputation for granting forgiveness. It was as if Jesus was on probation and, therefore, it was not necessary to bestow the foot washing, oil anointing and ceremonial kiss on him since he was not worthy to receive them. I think that Simon was hoping that he could catch Jesus in something wrong just so that he could make a spectacle of him and he would not have wanted to admit that he openly and correctly welcomed him. It is also very likely that this was a very pretentious affair, and it was Simon's goal for people to see what a wonderful person he was, especially when he exposed Jesus as a fool. Little did he know who would be shown up as the fool!

2. ***The woman went straight for Jesus when she entered the room, not speaking to anyone. Name two reasons why she might have been so focused.***

This woman had heard of Jesus. She, like so many others, had felt his gentleness, heard his teachings and wanted to believe that he really did have a message of healing, forgiveness and restoration for everyone. She would have heard him speak of his father's wonderful kingdom in such a gripping way that she really could imagine herself as accepted into this kingdom of love.

This woman did not come to this function for good conversation and good food—after all, she knew that no one really wanted to see her there. She did not come to please or anger any of those who knew her very well as something to be used and discarded until the next time. It was also no secret that those attending this party looked down on her as a dirty sinner. I think the first reason that she was so focused on Jesus was because she was completely broken and bruised and wanted someone to love her—really love her—just as she was. After all that she had done and had done to her, she was far too weak and fragile to be able to pick herself up, brush off and start over again. Even though she came in so broken, she felt that she could see a glimmer of light at the end of the road and she desperately wanted to reach it.

The second reason this woman was so focused was that she had come to worship him. To display her worship, she brought with her a box full of perfume and, for her, it was very expensive perfume. Her worship was expressed as thanksgiving to Jesus. She brought it as a gift and she was determined that she would give it to him. It may also have been in the back of her mind that she had to give it to him quickly in case the others threw her out. Simon was probably thinking about what to do with her but then thought Jesus would take care of it himself, and take care of it he did—Jesus accepted her act of worship and forgave her of her sins.

5. ***Make a list of some of the emotions that might have engulfed this woman.***

Fear, love, excitement and passion for Jesus, as well as overwhelming joy for the forgiveness that she received and the new life that she could now begin.

6. ***What were the four steps that she followed as she met Jesus?***

She washed his feet with her tears, dried them with her hair, covered his feet with kisses and poured oil over them.

7. ***What would the Pharisees have been thinking of her and of Jesus because he did not send her away like they thought he would?***

The Pharisees must have been so shocked at the sight that they weren't sure what to do. Their eyes kept watching Simon to see if he was going to do anything other than sit there dumbfounded. They may have felt that this was some kind of a joke and hoped that Jesus would see it too, but he only felt compassion for this woman.

12. ***We may think of worship as singing songs in church but there are many other ways to worship God. Read these verses and then describe other methods of worship that are noted.***

(It is interesting to note that the word "worship" appears 188 times in the King James Version.)

Psalm 29:2—stand and give praise to him.

Psalm 95:6—bow down, and kneel or fall prostrate before him.

Psalm 99:5—the lifting of hands and kneeling before God; giving him glory and praise by exalting him.

In addition to these three scriptures, we need to remember that the act of worship is one of being in a relationship with God. To begin, we must prepare our hearts to come into the presence of the Most High. We must ask him to forgive us for any wrongdoing against his commands and ask for his mercy and grace to cover us. We then need to come into the heavenly realm where we can converse with God.

Acts of worship have been looked at as the giving of gifts, and when we worship God, we are giving ourselves over to him for his pleasure as a gift. The method or position of how we worship isn't as important as doing it. God longs for you to bring your praise to him no matter if you are sitting, standing or falling prostrate. He doesn't care if you are walking, riding a bike, standing in your room, in church or if you are driving your car.

13

Looking to the Future

Chapter Objective

Each of us is valuable and necessary to God and the work of his Kingdom.

Future Study Focus

God can do the work himself, but he wants us to join with him to further his Kingdom. We all have a part to play and we need to be ready and willing to do it.

Questions

1. *Search your concordance and find as many scriptures as you can that remind you of God's plan such as:*

    Psalm 33:11

    Proverbs 16:1, 19:21

    Isaiah 44:13

    Jeremiah 29:11, 49:20 and 50:45

What I have learned

Now it is your turn to take what you have learned here and move onward and outward for the Lord. Remember to study his Word and listen carefully for the direction of the Holy Spirit.

With him guiding you, I know you can do it! Have fun and make trouble for the devil!

Max Lucado, *You Are Special.* copyright 1997 Crossway Books a division of Good News Publishers

Max Lucado, *In the Eye of the Storm*, (Nashville: Word Publishing, 1991) ch. 23.

"One Flaw In Women" (Author Unknown)

"You Are the Heart Of Me."; Performed by Kathy Troccoli, written by Ty Lacy, Sam Mizell & Steve Siler, 2002 EMI April Music/Ty Me A River Music/ASCAP.

Barbara Johnson Books, W Publishing Group, Thomas Nelson Inc.

C. Peter Wagner, *Your Spiritual Gifts Can Help Your Church Grow* (Ventura, CA: Regal Books, 2005).

Florence Littauer, *Personality Plus: How to Understand Others by Understanding Yourself*, (Grand Rapids: Fleming H. Revell, 1992).

Adapted from Caroline Whitbeck; Plato, *Timaeus* 90e; 'Theories of Sex Difference', in Gould and Wartofsky (eds.), *Women and Philosophy*, New York

1976, pp. 54-80; M. Maloney, 'The Arguments for Women's Difference in Classical Philosophy and Early Christianity', pp. 41-49.

Eliezer Seagal, *Jewish Free Press,* October 21, 1999, p. 10

Patsy Clairmont, *Sportin' a 'Tude,* (Colorado Springs: Focus on the Family Publishing, 1996).

Merriam-Webster's Online Dictionary©2008 by Merriam-Webster, Incorporated (www.Merriam-Webster.com).

"Sea of Forgetfulness", Helen Baylor, as recorded on the *I Will Be Free* album published by Women of Faith, 2007.

Reference only, Thelma Wells, Women of God Ministries with Thelma Wells, 2005. www.thelmawells.com

Reference only, Liz Curtis Higgs, Liz Cutis Higgs, an Encourager, 2005. www.lizcurtishiggs.com

Reference only, Mother Theresa, Nobleprize.org, 2005

"I am Woman", Helen Reddy and Ray Burton, Capital Records, 1973.

Tyrone Williams, as presented to Canada Arise Youth Night, Calgary, AB, Canada, 2001.

"Spirit of the Living God," Words and Music by Daniel Iverson, Moody Press, 1935/1963.

Reference only, Barbra Streisand http://www.barbrastreisand.com/us/home

CPSIA information can be obtained at www.ICGtesting.com
Printed in the USA
LVOW052239270812

296181LV00001B/1/P